THE DEVIL TO PAY

THE DEVIL TO PAY

BEING the famous HISTORY OF JOHN FAUSTUS the Conjurer of Wittenberg in Germany ; how he sold his immortal soul to the Enemy of Mankind, and was served XXIV years by Mephistopheles, and obtained Helen of Troy to his paramour, with many other marvels ; and how GOD dealt with him at the last.

A Stage-Play

by DOROTHY L. SAYERS

WIPF & STOCK · Eugene, Oregon

Wipf and Stock Publishers
199 W 8th Ave, Suite 3
Eugene, OR 97401

The Devil Pay
By Sayers, Dorothy L.
Copyright©1939 by Sayers, Dorothy L.
ISBN 13: 978-1-61097-020-4
Publication date: 8/1/2011
Previously published by Victor Gollancz Ltd, 1939

HARCOURT WILLIAMS

*"What I have done is yours ; what I have to do is
yours ; being part in all I have, devoted yours."*

Sound without ear is but an airy stirring,
Light without eyes, but an obscure vibration,
Souls' conference, solitude, and no conferring,
Till it by senses find interpretation ;
Gold is not wealth but by the gift and taking,
Speech without mind is only passing vapour ;
So is the play, save by the actor's making,
No play, but dull, deaf, senseless ink and paper.

Either for either made: light, eye ; sense, spirit ;
Ear, sound ; gift, gold ; play, actor ; speech and knowing,
Become themselves by what themselves inherit
From their sole heirs, receiving and bestowing ;
Thus, then, do thou, taking what thou dost give,
Live in these lines, by whom alone they live.

Dedicated to the Dorothy L. Sayers Society
that has generously sponsored
the production
of this 2011 series edition

For more information about the DLS Society
please turn to the last page of this book

Introduction to the 2011 Series Edition

On the occasion of the republication of some of Dorothy Leigh Sayers' plays, we pay tribute to a most remarkable person: a literary entrepreneur of no mean order, a lay theologian in an age when it was almost unthinkable for a woman to be acknowledged as a theologian, a thinker who pioneered new ways of engaging audiences with central Christian dogmas as rehearsed in the Church's creeds. The final flowering of her work was connected with her rediscovery of Dante's *Divine Comedy*, which stimulated her to produce some of her finest work, including the play she personally thought was her very best. She did not set out to be a writer of 'religious' drama, but her experience of life through a traumatic era of European history, together with her special talents, made such drama part of her legacy to us.

Born in 1893 at the tail-end of the Victorian era, Dorothy was the only child of well-educated parents. She was baptised in Christ Church, Oxford, (Diocesan Cathedral as well as College Chapel) where her father, an ordained clergyman of the Church of England, was Headmaster of the school which educated the boys who sang in the choir. In 1897 her father accepted a Christ Church living in the 'Fens' (drained, hedgeless farmland) about sixteen miles from Cambridge, and together with her mother, a series of governesses and a brief experience of school from age fifteen, she received an excellent education which suited her particular talents. She emerged into adulthood holding to a number of strong convictions, one of which was about the importance of vigorous and clear thinking and speaking about Christian dogma, enlivening the real and varied existences of human beings in all their complexity. Entry to Somerville

College, Oxford in 1912 placed DLS among a very favoured few in the Britain of her day, though privilege sheltered no one from the miseries of World War 1 as some of her early published poetry reveals. In any event, her 'Hymn in Contemplation of Sudden Death' (1916)[1] transcends its origins in wartime, though was to come into its own especially in the appalling era of aerial bombing of civilians in the new horrors of World War 11. This is of central importance for the cathedral play written for Lichfield, as we shall see.

So far as World War I is concerned, DLS' detective fiction reflects something of the world of the survivors and the bereaved, and we note here that she never isolated herself from the social and political struggles of her day. Some of her sensitivities are displayed in the development of her portrait of her aristocratic sleuth, Peter Wimsey. He struggles with 'shell-shock' and the memory of having had to give orders which sent so many to their deaths, and as a sleuth he is responsible too for other deaths in a country which still enforced capital punishment. A priority for DLS of course was to find ways of earning her own living, whilst also negotiating a series of love-relationships amongst the somewhat problematic selection of available men of her social class and education post-1918. A man who was not 'marriageable' became the father of her son, her only child, and she simply had to earn money to support Anthony, brought up as he was by a trusted friend before he came to know Dorothy as his birth-mother rather than as his 'adoptive' mother. In 1926 DLS married in a Registry Office a divorced war-veteran, 'Mac', whose children from his first marriage did not live with him.

Life was far from easy, what with the political and economic legacy of World War I to contend with, and the lack of sheer political will to make changes for the general good. Few could

---

1 In the selection Hone, R.E.(ed) *Poetry of Dorothy L. Sayers*, Dorothy L. Sayers Society, Swavesey, Cambridge, 1996, pp.78-79; and in Loades, A. (ed) *Dorothy L. Sayers. Spiritual Writings*, SPCK, London, 1993, pp.10-11 from her Opus 1.

view the possibility of yet another major conflict with other than the gravest misgivings. Yet it became imperative to destroy the 'Third Reich' with the consequences for the shape of post-war Europe emerging in the latter part of DLS' lifetime. She contributed vigorously to the thinking about the future which needed to be undertaken to bring about change both for the majority of the British population and for international relationships, not least those with defeated countries. Her detective fiction was by no means a trivial distraction from these important tasks, for in it she expressed some of her most passionately held convictions. For central to Christian faith is unequivocal commitment to truth and justice, without these being identified as specifically Christian in her novels. Thus when on honeymoon with Harriet (*Busman's Honeymoon* (1937) she and Peter together face the fact they cannot pick and choose, that they must have the truth no matter who suffers, and that nothing else matters. This will result in a death sentence for the murderer, and another agonising night for Peter as he waits for the eight a.m. moment of the execution, and who knows what consequences for others involved, however marginally. Human justice and the pursuit of truth will never be simple, and the aftermath unpredictable, hardly free of ambiguity and even of a measure of injustice. As Peter says, 'If there *is* a God or a judgement – what next? What have we done?'

God and judgement were precisely to become the focus of her attention when DLS was caught up into the orbit of Canterbury Cathedral and its Festival of Music and Drama. It was the 'drama' to be associated with the Festival which made it exceptional for its day, given the long-standing suspicion of the pre-Reformation traditions of theatre and liturgy almost wiped out by certain kinds of Protestantism. Canterbury happened to have as its Dean G.K.A. Bell, during the period when its Chapter (governing body) came to think it was time to challenge that suspicion. Having in 1927 founded the Friends of Canterbury Cathedral (an initiative to be followed in many other cathedrals) he found himself with an ally in the person of Margaret Babington, who became the Friends' Steward the following year. Chapter and Friends made possible plays specially commissioned to be performed on the cathedral premises, continuing even after Bell has become Bishop of Chichester in 1929. [2] Bell remains important for understanding DLS' perspective on the cost of the Allied victory in World War II since he became a passionate critic of some aspects of the government's conduct of the war as an Episcopal member of the Upper House of Parliament (the 'Lords').

Both before and after Bell's time as Dean, the plays commissioned for Canterbury Cathedral were by a very distinguished lineage of writers, with T.S. Eliot's *Murder in the Cathedral* (1935) having a most profound impact, given that it was written for the Cathedral in which Thomas a` Becket had been done to death. It also reminded audiences of the possibility of continuing conflict between monarch/government and bishop. Following his own contribution on Thomas Cranmer, it was Charles Williams no less who suggested DLS as writer of a play for Canterbury, a choice not necessarily as surprising as some seem to have thought. She had some experience of stage performance and stagecraft from both school and university and a brief experience of school teaching. She had published a short 'poetic drama' *The Mocking of Christ* in her collection of *Catholic Tales and Christian Songs* (1918); *Busman's Honeymoon* had first seen the light of day as a play for the stage (1936), co-authored with another Somervillian, writer Muriel St Clare Byrne, distinguished historian and writer and lecturer at the Royal College of Dramatic Art, and one of DLS' valuable friends in the theatrical world. It was a singular challenge in itself to hit on a subject relevant to Canterbury, and this DLS triumphantly did in choosing to write about the rebuilding of the Cathedral Choir after the fire of 1174, chronicled by a

2. Jasper, R.C.D. *George Bell: Bishop of Chichester,* OUP, London, 1967. See also Pickering, K. *Drama in the Cathedral. The Canterbury Festival Plays 1928-1948* Churchman Publishing, Worthing, 1985.

monk, Gervase. Thus *The Zeal of Thy House* came into being, first performed between 12-18 June, 1937, in the Cathedral, and on a London stage in March 1938.

In *Zeal,* some of DLS' convictions are made clear, notably in the character of the architect, William of Sens, the embodiment of the principal human sin, pride. The play is also significant for comprehending the significance for DLS of good work of whatever kind, and her grasp of what it means for human persons to acknowledge themselves as creative agents in the image of the divine Trinity. All this most painfully William has to learn. From this point on, some characteristic features of her work in drama began to emerge. Music specially written for her plays was integral to the liveliness of her presentation of Christian dogma, that in turn further heightened in some cases her scenes of debate and argument, testing vitally important judgements about the truth of a situation. Further, her new mode of success as a dramatist was in part the result of her personal humility, willing to take the expert advice of producers and actors as to what would and would not work 'on stage', however admirably written. She was always constructively involved in her productions, in every possible way, making 'cuts' as rehearsals proceeded, whilst frequently restoring her text for publication. Text not used in the original production might or might not be fruitfully used in subsequent ones, depending on context, which might be quite different from its first production.

Such was the success of *Zeal* that DLS was invited to write on Christian dogma for major newspapers, and in addition, received a commission from the then immensely prestigious BBC for a Nativity play (*He That Should Come*) to be broadcast on Christmas Day, 1938. It needs to be recalled that broadcasting was relatively new as a medium for large-scale communication to audiences, and the BBC had high expectations of what it should and should not present to its listeners. Of prime importance for DLS was that she conveyed to her listeners that Christ was born 'into the world', into 'real life', and she had to convey this by sound only. So she re-imagined the world into which Christ was born, engaging not merely with the relevant initial chapters of the first and third gospels (Matthew and Luke) but with centuries of enjoyment of and reflection on the narratives and what had been perceived to be their significance. The main setting is the common courtyard of an inn, in which the characters DLS introduces can grumble about absolutely anything, with differing points of view to be expected from a Pharisee, a merchant and a centurion for example. Joseph plays a central role, and from the world beyond the courtyard the shepherds appear, and it is their gifts which are presented to the child newly born. Finally, we may note that as the published text of her Nativity play makes clear, DLS had not been intimidated by criticism that 'long speeches' would be unintelligible to her audiences, since she went on writing them, whilst allowing for them to be 'cut'. Much would depend on audiences and performers, and she had high expectations of all of them.

So successful was *He That Should Come* 'on air', indeed, that DLS was able to respond to a major challenge, namely, the writing of twelve radio plays (the first broadcast of which began on 21 December, 1941) entitled *The Man Born to be King*. These plays remain unique in their conception and execution, not least in wartime, and her vigorous introduction to the published version expounded her intentions as a writer in respect of 'the life of the God Incarnate' which gives us further insight into her theology. Christ 'on air' had to be credible, and so had the particular human beings with whom he had dealings, right through to the scenes when the risen Christ meets with his disciples, surely a major challenge for any dramatist. There were objections in advance of the broadcasts to listeners being able to hear the 'voice' of Jesus of Nazareth', but the fuss gave the plays excellent publicity, and they have remained a most moving exploration of the Gospels and their significance. Interestingly, given that she had limited the presence of the 'Kings' in *He That Should Come* to the 'Prologue' and the very last minutes of that play, in *The Man born to be King* she seized the opportunity further to explore their significance in the very first play of the twelve, 'Kings in Judea'.

That apart, there is an important thread of connection to notice which links DLS' exploration of the character of William in *Zeal* to the 1941 *The Man Born to be King*. William's principal sin was that of pride; that is also true of Judas according to her brilliant analysis and portrayal of him in *The Man Born to be King*. Between these two productions one further attempt to explore the roots of human sin in pride had presented itself in *The Devil to Pay*, first performed in Canterbury Cathedral 10-17 June, 1939, with a run on a London stage in the next month. (The outbreak of war in the first days of September was to cut short any further production at least for the time being). Writing this play may well have sharpened up DLS' perception of Judas and of Christ's dealings with him. The theme of *The Devil to Pay* is a re-working of the legend of Faustus- hardly easy to handle. In the first place it had no particular connection with Canterbury Cathedral. In the second place it could be very difficult to persuade an audience to take the 'devil' seriously as the personification of evil, for he was likely to be so entertaining as to 'upstage' the other characters, most importantly, that of Faustus with his besetting sin of pride. DLS had the courage to tackle the legend, because she saw in Faustus a figure which we might say was all too familiar in the political culture of her day, though she does not explicitly make the connection. For we can see behind her Faustus not just the 'impulsive reformer' in all his impatience, but the arrogance of the dictator who turns to unbridled violence as well as to fantasy, with incalculable harm as the result. Her attempt to tackle the full scope of Christ's atonement and redemption lay ahead of her, but there was at least one clue as to her confidence in print, for in her 1916 'The Gates of Paradise', DLS had written of the arrival of Judas accompanied by Christ himself at 'Hades gate' (alluding to the ancient tradition of Christ's raid upon those in bondage to Satan)[3]. It is important to bear this in mind to understand the final scene of *Devil*. Here she has Mephistopheles put in charge of the purging of Faustus and the destruction of the evil for which he has been responsible, but with Faustus himself secure in the promise of his Judge that he will never be forsaken, and that he will be met by his Judge/Saviour at the gates of hell. DLS never denies the depths of human wickedness, but hangs on to a trust in 'redemption' on the very eve of war, of a scope and ferocity she and others at this stage could only fear.

In retrospect, it seems extraordinary, given the progress of World War II in its early stages, that anyone should have had the confidence to suppose that there should be serious consideration given to the shape of social and political life after the war, but to that consideration DLS indeed made a contribution. Thus, for example, in her essay in aesthetics and theology, her 1941 *The Mind of the Maker*, a major point is that if human dignity is to be respected, then social, political and economic life must be so ordered as to express human imagination and creativity. This conviction she spelled out in a series of notably pungent essays. Wartime, however, provoked her into writing one play with which she was richly satisfied, and that was to be *The Just Vengeance* of 1946. The maturity of her theological and dramatic vision now flowered in a play entirely original to herself, born of a number of factors. There was the stimulus Charles Williams' gave to her thinking with his 1943 *The Figure of Beatrice* (Williams himself sadly dying at the tail-end of the war). The result was her re-reading and translation of the whole of Dante's *Divine Comedy*, sometimes working away at this in air-raid shelters. And at this juncture DLS was presented with yet another opportunity to write for a Cathedral. In 1943 it was far from clear when the war might end, or on what terms, but the Chapter of Lichfield Cathedral had the vision and courage

3. See Loades, *Dorothy L. Sayers. Spiritual Writings*, pp.12-15 from her Opus 1.

to advance plans for a service of Thanksgiving for the preservation of the Cathedral, and a Pageant to celebrate seven hundred and fifty years since its foundation, which fell in 1945. Given the inevitable austerities of wartime and its aftermath, it is unsurprising that the whole celebration could not take place in the anniversary year. The invitation to DLS to write a play for Lichfield gave her a priceless opportunity to relate Dante's vision to some deeply troubling features of her own era. (In addition to the play, her appropriation of Dante was to speak most powerfully to the reading public in the years after the war, made possible by the inclusion of her work on 'Hell' and 'Purgatory' in the new Penguin Classics series). It was in Canto xxi of 'Purgatory' that she found the phrase which became the title of *The Just Vengeance*, first performed June 15-26, 1946.

The importance of the phrase was to become clear as DLS wrote *The Just Vengeance*. No pacifist, she had come to the conclusion that the war simply had to be endured. That said, she and others had to reckon with a new dimension of war, which was the deliberate targeting of civilian populations from the air. As World War II developed, Bishop Bell for one became a serious critic of the policy which aimed at the systematic destruction of major German cities one by one, in order to bring the war to an end. For DLS there was a personal dimension to the matter of the bombing of civilians, however. She had learned much from Fraülein Fehmer, a music teacher at school, who had returned home to Frankfurt and become an ardent Nazi. DLS' poem 'Target Area' (1940) imagines her former teacher under the airborne onslaught, rightly recognising that in willing the war she willed the means, though their full horror was yet to be discovered. [4]

The issues she had to some extent explored in her detective fiction DLS now confronted in the light of Christian dogma, that is, that the divine court the human judges as well as the accused alike stand before God, that we are none of us free of guilt. Specifically in *The Just Vengeance* she set herself the task

4. Hone, *Poetry,* pp. 140-145.

of portraying the Christian doctrine of redemption in the light of the conduct of the war. She set the action in a moment of time as an airman is shot down from his bomber, whilst drawing him into the whole company of those who have and continue to inhabit Lichfield. What she wanted above all to convey was what Dante himself had explored in his understanding of 'just vengeance' in the third and final 'Paradise' section of his *Comedy*. This is that 'redemption', if embraced, leads the sanctified to experience the grace, joy and delight of salvation beyond agony and horror. This third section of Dante DLS knew very thoroughly, and drew on it throughout her play, though never completed her own translation and commentary on it before her own death in 1957. Thus *The Just Vengeance* yields irreplaceable insight into how she imagined the significance of 'redemption' for her own time. The popularity of 'Hell' in the immediate post-war period was understandable – the wicked getting their 'come-uppance' as it were; but the challenge of understanding 'redemption' was the greater. She rose to it magnificently, and was justifiably deeply satisfied with the result.

DLS by this time could draw on long-sustained friendships and trust with the professional actors and theatre people who had worked with her pre-war, with all involved surmounting the difficulties of securing and re-working needed materials in very short supply. Music was integral to the effectiveness of the production, and most fortunately she engaged the skills in costume and scene design of Norah Lambourne, with her extensive first-hand experience of theatre productions (in the 1950s crucial to the re-staging of the York Mystery Plays). She was also a key player in the production of DLS' final play, for another commemorative occasion. When Mac, DLS' husband died in 1950, Nora Lambourne moved in with DLS, becoming an invaluable collaborator for *The Emperor Constantine* first performed on Monday 2 July, 1951.

If writing a play for somewhere the size of Lichfield Cathedral was a challenge, an even more problematic context was the Colchester cinema in Festival of Britain year (1951) for Colchester's own festival contribution. The connection of Colchester with Constantine was through a legend which claimed that his mother, Helena, was the daughter of its King, Coel, DLS accepted no restrictions on the size of the cast, nor the time needed to perform the whole play (well over three hours), which displays the complexities of Constantine's achievement and exercise of imperial power, including the debate about Christ's relationship to God at the Council of Nicaea in 325 AD, under Constantine's personal aegis. DLS did not spare her audience the inevitable conflicts of the imperial court, leading to the tragedy of Constantine's destruction of his son. Act 3 is the key, performed in London as *Christ's Emperor*. Like William of Sens, Judas, Faust and the bomber pilot, Constantine has most painfully to realise that the cleansing and redemption of his life comes about through Christ, and that is the precisely the consequence of the dogma he had been instrumental in establishing at Nicaea. It is his mother, Helena, who mediates this truth to him. The play may well be said to be of wider significance exhibiting the problems of connecting the dogmas of a church upheld by state authority, with political life and its associated miseries and triumphs. In its London context of St Thomas' Church off Regent Street the shorter version (*Christ's* Emperor) was set for a challenging run, but the death of George VI in its very first week put paid to it. Age-old issues about the human pursuit of truth and justice all too evidently remain.

DLS' work in many genres continued until her unexpected death in 1957. It is thanks to the initiative of Wipf & Stock that we have the texts of these six productions re-published in single volume format, sponsored by the Dorothy L. Sayers Society. Everyone owes an inestimable debt to Dr Barbara Reynolds, engaged life-long with the work of Dante, with DLS' appropriation of Dante, completing the 'Paradise' section of the *Comedy* after DLS' death, editing her letters, writing her biography, and in so many ways stimulating interest in the whole range of work of a most remarkable human being.

The 'religious' plays of DLS, devised for cathedrals, stages and broadcasts were written to be adaptable for performance in many different contexts. They are meant to be exciting, stirring, challenging, memorable, getting everyone involved at the most serious level with issues of inescapable and permanent importance.

Ann Loades
Tayport, Scotland
April 2011

Synopses of the Religious Drama by Dorothy Sayers

THE ZEAL OF THY HOUSE

Dorothy L. Sayers took her inspiration from a monk's account of the fire of 1174, and the subsequent rebuilding of Canterbury Cathedral Quire. She portrays William of Sens, the chosen architect, as eaten away by pride in his splendid work, unable to give glory to God for his achievement. Enacted in the presence of a group of graciously influential Archangels, the play reveals the carelessness of some of the monks, resulting in the terrifying fall that cripples William. His agony brings him to repentance and gratitude before God, and finally to the renunciation of his role, leaving the completion of the re-building to others.

First performed on June 12, 1937; first published by V. Gollancz in June 1937.

HE THAT SHOULD COME

In this first of her plays for religious broadcasting, Dorothy L. Sayers wanted to convince listeners of the truth that Christ was born into our deeply problematic world, in his case, in territory overrun by an army of occupation. Although framed as it were by the voices of the three 'wise men' asking whether the birth of a particular child could possibly fulfil their desires, the focus of the play is on the conflict of opinion (about roads, taxes, and so forth) expressed by those in the courtyard of the inn at Bethlehem.

Joseph is given a most significant role, and it is the shepherds whose gifts are presented when the Holy Family is revealed.

First broadcast on December 25, 1938; first published by V. Gollancz in November 1939.

THE DEVIL TO PAY

Dorothy L. Sayers re-worked the legend of Faust as a serious 'comedy', presenting Faust as one who chooses wicked means as an end to an admirable goal: the relief of suffering (while becoming entirely focussed on his own supposed satisfactions). In the last scene, in the Court of Heaven, Azrael, angel of the souls of the dead, claims Faustus' soul, opposing Mephistopheles' claim. With the knowledge of good and evil returned to him, Faustus finally accepts that his evil must be cleansed, with Mephistopheles serving as the agent of that purgation. Faustus accepts his need for cleansing, trusting that the divine Judge/Court President, will indeed in mercy meet him at the very gates of hell, finally redeemed.

First performed on June 10, 1939; first published by V. Gollancz in June 1939.

THE MAN BORN TO BE KING

In twelve plays for broadcasting at monthly intervals, Dorothy L. Sayers drew on material from all four Gospels, keeping the theme of Jesus of Nazareth's divine kingship in focus throughout, while locating him firmly in the social and political context of his time. The first half cover episodes that precede the final journey to Jerusalem and the latter half primarily deal with Passion Week themes. It is on the simplicity and profundity of Jesus' words in the Fourth Gospel especially that Sayers drew on in her own writing for the 'voice' of Jesus 'on air'. The plays gave her an opportunity to explore the many gospel characters surrounding Jesus, not least that of Judas. And beyond the utter sorrow of Jesus' death, the King comes into his own in the garden of resurrection.

The first play was broadcast on December 21, 1941, with the rest at four-weekly intervals thereafter, concluding on October 18, 1942; first published by V. Gollancz in 1943.

THE JUST VENGEANCE

In this play Dorothy L. Sayers addressed the crimes and problems of human life, especially those of the victors in war, in an entirely novel way, by precipitating an airman in the very moment of his death back into the company of citizens of the 'City', in this case, Lichfield. The citizens range from Adam and Eve (Adam himself the inventor of the axe which kills Abel) together with other biblical characters in the history of redemption brought to new life as members of the City, (e.g. Judas is a common informer). Others bear burdens of shame, toil, fear, poverty and ingratitude. Former inhabitants (e.g. George Fox, Dr. Johnson) help the airman to see that no more than they can he shift the burden of his guilt and grief that they all share. There is but one remedy, to join the 'Persona Dei' carrying his cross, finding indeed that he bears their burdens for them. The 'Persona Dei' is finally seen in resurrection and glory.

First performed on June 15, 1946; first published by V. Gollancz in June 1946. Broadcast: March 30, 1947.

THE EMPEROR CONSTANTINE

A brief 'Prologue' by the 'Church' introduces the career of Constantine (from A.D. 305-337) with scenes from the empires of both west and east, concentrating on Constantine's progress to imperial power and inevitably in religious belief. He discovers Christ to be the God who has made him his earthly vice-regent as single Emperor. Summoning the Council of Nicaea at 325, an invigorating debate results in the acceptance of Constantine's formula that Christ is 'of one substance with God'. The implications of the creed of Nicaea are revealed in the last part of the play in which it is his mother, Helena, who brings him to the realisation that he needs redemption by Christ for his political and military life as well as for the domestic tragedy which has resulted in the death of his son.

First performed on July 2, 1951; first published by V. Gollancz in August 1951. A shortened version entitled *Christ's Emperor* was performed at St Thomas' Church, Regent Street in February 1952.

PREFACE

In my previous Canterbury play, *The Zeal of Thy House,* the problem was to supply a supernatural interpretation of a piece of human history. In the present play, the problem is exactly reversed: it is a question of supplying some kind of human interpretation of a supernatural legend. This means that the supernatural elements in the two stories have called for quite different handling. In the former case, they affected only the moral, and not the machinery, of the fable; take away the visible angels, and the course of William of Sens's fall and repentance remains essentially unaltered. But in whatever way we retell the tale of Faustus, the supernatural element *is* the story. For the " two-hours' traffic of our stage," we must indulge in the " willing suspension of disbelief." We must accept magic and miracle as physical realities; we must admit the possibility of genuine witchcraft, of the strange legal transaction by which a man might sell his soul to Satan, of the actual appearance of the Devil in concrete bodily shape. The Faustus legend is dyed in grain with the thought and feeling of its period; nothing could be more characteristic than its odd jumble of spirituality and crude superstition; of scripture and classical myth; of Catholic theology and anti-clerical humanism; of the adventurous passion for, and the timorous distrust of learning. We may put what allegorical or symbolical construction we like on this fantastical piece of diabolism; but to enjoy it as drama, we must contrive to put ourselves back in spirit to the opening years of the sixteenth century. Accordingly, the better to induce this frame of mind in the spectator, I have deliberately reverted to the setting and machinery of the early Renaissance stage, with its traditional " mansions," its conventional Heaven and Hell-mouth, and its full apparatus of diabolical masquerade.

The picturesque figure of the Devil has a perennial attraction for the playwright, although, theologically speaking, he is apt to make hay of any story into which he intrudes. The fact is, the Devil is a character of very mixed origin; as Mrs. Malaprop would say, he is, " like Cerberus, three gentlemen at once." There is, to begin with, the " fallen seraph " of ancient

Talmudic tradition; the rebel created for better things, and suffering torment in everlasting exile from God's presence. It is his dark angelic melancholy that makes the splendour of Marlowe's Mephistopheles and Milton's Satan. Under whatever name he appears, this personage is but one among an uncounted legion of the lost. Although the existence of a chief devil is postulated (whether called Satan, Lucifer, Beelzebub or what not), each evil spirit is conceived of as being a separate personality, rather than summing up in himself the essence of all evil.

Secondly, and inextricably confused, by name and exploits, with the conception of the fallen angels, we have " the Devil " —the absolute spirit of Evil, set over against God, who is the absolute Good. His origin appears to be Persian, and he properly belongs to that dualistic cosnogony which divides the rulership of the world equally between light and darkness, Ormuzd and Ahriman. In Mediaeval theatrical practice, any devil one may choose to bring upon the stage is apt to assume this generalised character of incarnate Evil, whatever references he may make to his diabolic superiors, and however many demonic companions he may summon to his assistance. For the purpose of dramatic symbolism one has to assume that any devil may symbolise " the Devil," and be treated accordingly. Goethe's Mephistopheles has this universality of evil; and in him the poet typifies his own conception of what Evil is, " *der Geist der stets verneint.*"

Thirdly, there is the " merry devil "—a mocking spirit, who probably derives, complete with horn and hoof, from the classical Pan and his satyrs. This lively personage endeared himself deeply to the Mediaeval playgoer, who, in any performance of religious drama, confidently looked forward to the Devil as the " comic turn." Squibs and crackers and poltergeist antics were always part of " Old Hornie's " repertoire; and thus we find the stately Mephistopheles of Marlowe condescending to play vulgar tricks upon the Pope and souse a Horse-courser in a dirty pond. That kind of thing was expected of the Devil, and, had it been omitted from the play, the pit would no doubt have demanded its money back. Trickery and mischief fit in more appropriately with the character of Goethe's Mephistopheles than with Marlowe's; and indeed, towards the end of the long second part of *Faust*, it becomes difficult to remember that the Devil is the father of all Evil; he bears so strong an appearance of being merely an amiable gentleman with a slightly sardonic sense of humour. But indeed, as Marlowe, Milton, Goethe, and every other writer who has meddled with the Devil has discovered, the chief difficulty is to prevent this sympathetic character from becoming the hero of the story.

It is hopeless, at this time of day, to disentangle the stage presentation of the Devil from its inherited inconsistencies, or to make every detail of it fit neatly into a rigid theological system. Nor is it possible to do away altogether with the inherent unreason that attends the practice of Art Magic. If, as we are so often told, religion and magic were formed out of the same raw material, nothing could be more remarkable and impressive than the difference, in the finished article, between the rational severity of the one and the incoherent irrationality of the other. It must be remembered that the Mediaeval magician did not, generally speaking, set to work to call up devils in the name of Beelzebub; he called them up in the name of the Trinity. However sordid, vile or ridiculous the end for which he summoned the spirits, the ultimate sanction invoked to attain that end was the power of God and His angels. In the very act of denying and defying God, he surrounded himself with every protection that the name of God could afford against the consequences of the act. In their more blasphemous excesses, his conjurations were spells, explicitly compelling God, by the power of His own name, to perform the conjurer's will. It is this curious dissociation of the power from the source of power that characterises magic as opposed to sacrament. The magical power is, in fact, considered to inhere in the divine name itself, and to operate automatically and independently of the divine authority. Thus the ancient manuals of conjuration present us with the somewhat inconsequent spectacle of a magician urgently calling upon God to protect and assist him in the carrying-out of such agreeable little bedevilments as the diseasing of his neighbour's cattle, the debauching of his neighbour's wife, or even the consort and enjoyment of delectable she-devils in bodily form. Whether, indeed, a generation so addicted as our own to the cherishing of mascots and the reckless abuse of ideological formulae is entitled to cast the stone of scorn at its Mediaeval forbears is matter for consideration.

But when we have allowed for all its fantastical trappings and illogical absurdities, the legend of Faustus remains one of the great stories of the world; a perpetual fascination to the poet, whose task it is to deal with the eternities. For at the base of it lies the question of all questions: the nature of Evil and its place in the universe. Symbolise Evil, and call it the Devil, and then ask how the Devil comes to be. Is he, as the Manichees taught, a power co-equal with and opposed to God? Or, if God is all-powerful, did He make the Devil, and if so, why, and with what justification? Is the Devil a positive force, or merely a negation, the absence of Good? In what sense can a man be said to sell his soul to the Devil? What kind of man might do so, and, above all, for what inducement? Further, what meaning are we to place upon the concept of hell and damnation, with which the whole concept of the Devil is intimately bound up?

Questions such as these are answered by every generation in the light of its own spiritual needs and experience. And for each writer, when he has determined his own interpretation of the central mythus, there is, of course, the added technical interest of discovering how many features of the original legend offer themselves as valuable factors in his system of symbolism.

In the true spirit of the Renaissance, the legendary Faustus sells his soul for the satisfaction of intellectual curiosity and the lust of worldly power. Marlowe accepts those inducements as valid, and, though his sympathies are very much with Faustus, does not shrink from the tragical end of the story. Faustus is damned in accordance with the terms of the bond, and the sombre close of the drama is unrelieved by any ray of hope. In this play, there is scarcely any trace of the conventional Mediaeval hell of physical fire and brimstone; the famous speech of Mephistopheles embodies a purely spiritual concept of damnation:

> " *Why, this is hell, nor am I out of it.*
> *Think'st thou that I, who saw the face of God*
> *And tasted the eternal joys of Heaven,*
> *Am not tormented with ten thousand hells*
> *In being deprived of everlasting bliss?* "

For Goethe, it was impossible to accept the idea that desire for knowledge could be in itself an evil thing. Though Faustus signs the bond, Mephistopheles is cheated in the end, and Faustus goes to Heaven. This game of cheat-the-devil is in full accordance with the spirit of the early moralities; these often finish with a judgment scene, conducted by Our Lady in the strictest legal form, in which the Devil is tripped up over the terms of a compact, rather in the manner of Shylock in *The Merchant of Venice*. Goethe conceives of the Devil as a necessary part of God's plan for the world: he is the power " *der reizt und wirkt und muss als Teufel schaffen.*" The deadly sin is to give up striving and rest content, and the Devil is the irritant that keeps man at work. Goethe's Faust learns to use his infernal power to a good end, and finds contentment only in devotion to the service of man. It is while busily engaged in a work of public usefulness that he finds himself ready to say to the fleeting moment: " *Verweile doch, du bist so schön* "; and the comment of the angels is:

> " *Wer immer strebend sich bemüht
> Den können wir erlösen.*"

To endeavour to do again what greater poets have already magnificently done would be folly as well as presumption; and I have tried to offer a new presentment of Faustus. All other considerations apart, I do not feel that the present generation of English people needs to be warned against the passionate pursuit of knowledge for its own sake: that is not our besetting sin. Looking with the eyes of to-day upon that legendary figure of the man who bartered away his soul, I see in him the type of the impulsive reformer, over-sensitive to suffering, impatient of the facts, eager to set the world right by a sudden overthrow, in his own strength and regardless of the ineluctable nature of things. When he finds it is not to be done, he falls into despair (or, to use the current term, into " defeatism ") and takes flight into phantasy.

His escape takes a form very common in these times: it is the nostalgia of childhood, of the primitive, of the unconscious; the rejection of adult responsibility and the denial of all value to growth and time. Time has been exercising the minds of many writers of late. It has been suggested that it is pure illusion, or at most a cross-section of eternity, and that we may be comforted for the failures of our manhood by remembering that the youthful idealists we once were are our permanent and eternal selves. This doctrine is not really even consoling; since, if our youth is co-eternal with our age, then equally, our age is co-eternal with our youth; the corruptions of our ends poison our beginnings as certainly as the purity of our beginnings sanctifies our ends. The Church has always carefully distinguished time from eternity; as carefully as she has distinguished the Logos from the Father. It is true that we must become as little children and that " except a man be born again, he cannot see the kingdom of God." But that is not to be done by attempting to turn time backwards, or deny its validity in a material universe. " How can a man be born when he is old ? Can he enter the second time into his mother's womb and be born ? " The answer is that he cannot. " That which is born of the flesh is flesh, and that which is born of the spirit is spirit." Time and eternity are two different things, and that which exists temporally must admit the values of time. Against the exhortation to take refuge in infantilism we may set the saying of Augustine of Hippo concerning Christ: " *Cibus sum grandium; cresce et manducabis Me* "—" I am the food of the full-grown; become adult, and thou shalt feed on Me."

Has Evil any real existence, viewed *sub specie aeternitatis*? I have suggested that it has not; but that it is indissolubly linked with the concept of value in the material and temporal aspect of the universe. It is this issue which Faustus refuses to face; rather than grapple with the opposition of good and evil, he dissociates himself from common human experience. The results to his soul of this attempt to escape reality are displayed in a final judgment scene, where (with a rigid legal exactitude which, I feel sure, the Mediaeval mind would heartily approve) the Devil is cheated of his bond, but receives his precise due. The notion of the Devil as being set in charge of the place of purgation, as well as of the place in which all evil is consumed, was familiar enough to the Middle Ages, as is clearly seen in the Wakefield Pageant of *The Harrowing of Hell*, where Christ rebukes Satan in the words:

> " *I make no mastry but for myne,*
> *I wille theym save, that shalle the sow*
> *Thou hast no powere theym to pyne,*
> *Bot in my pryson for thare prow* [*profit*]."

Of the original Faustus legend, certain episodes are reproduced in some form or another in practically all treatments of the subject: Faustus' raising of Mephistopheles; his " disputations " with him concerning the nature of God; his twenty-four years' bond to Hell; his journeys to Rome, where he plays tricks upon the Pope, and to the Court of Charles V, where he assists the Imperial armies to achieve their victories in Italy; his having Helen of Troy for his paramour; and the final scene in which the Devil comes to claim his own. His servant, Christopher Wagner, is also traditional. One version recounts how Faustus sought to marry " a beautiful servant-girl," but was prevented by Mephistopheles, on the ground that marriage was a sacrament, and therefore an action pleasing to God and contrary to the terms of the bond. This episode forms the basis for the First Part of Goethe's *Faust*.

The central part of the story is chiefly taken up with a long series of disconnected marvels and miracles, mostly of a purely mischievous and puckish sort, as when Faustus swallows a wagon of hay and a span of horses, makes flowers bloom at Christmas, cuts off his own leg and restores it, draws wine from a table, or attends the Pope's banquet invisible and beats the guests about the head. None of this episodic material offers much opportunity to the dramatist for anything but " inexplicable dumb show and noise "; it is the beginning and the end of the tale that constitute its eternal appeal. In a version designed to be played in the restricted period of an hour and forty minutes, it has been necessary to exclude all merely episodic matter, and to concentrate on those incidents which are capable of being compressed into a reasonably coherent dramatic structure.

What Tophet is not Paradise, what Brimstone is not Amber, what gnashing is not a comfort, what gnawing of the worme is not a tickling, what torment is not a marriage bed to this damnation, to be secluded eternally, eternally, eternally, from the sight of God?

JOHN DONNE : Sermon preached to the Earle of Carlisle.

" *The Devil to Pay* " was originally produced in the Chapter House at the Canterbury Cathedral Festival, 10–17 June, 1939, under the management of the Friends of Canterbury Cathedral, with the following cast of professional and amateur players:

Wagner	PHILIP HOLLINGWORTH
Lisa	BETTY DOUGLAS
Faustus	HARCOURT WILLIAMS
Mephistopheles	FRANK NAPIER
Cardinal	CHARLES REEVES
Priest	WILLIAM FORDYCE
Pope	GEOFFREY KEABLE
Helen of Troy	MARY ALEXANDER
Young Faustus	ALASTAIR BANNERMAN
Azrael	STANLEY PINE
Emperor	WILLIAM FORDYCE
Empress	VERA COBURN FINDLAY
Chancellor	SIDNEY HAYNES
Secretary	MARSHALL HUGHES
Soul of Faustus	MAX WOOD
Judge	RAF DE LA TORRE

Devils : NIGEL BEARD — MICHAEL FOSTER — ANTHONY WARE — JOHN WILLIAMS

Citizens : PADDY FINN — KATHLEEN HETHERINGTON — RACHAEL HUBBLE — MAUD LISTER — JOAN POLLARD — EILEEN SHIPP — FRANK KIPPS — HOWARD OVERY — EDGAR PARKER-POPE — JACK VANE

Courtiers : FRANK KIPPS — JACK VANE

Page : DONALD FOSTER

Ladies : PADDY FINN — RACHAEL HUBBLE

The Music for the Songs and Final Chorus composed by
GERALD H. KNIGHT
Singers
String Orchestra
The Play produced by HARCOURT WILLIAMS
Scenery, Lighting and Stage Effects by FRANK NAPIER

34

PERSONS OF THE DRAMA
in the order of their appearing

CHRISTOPHER WAGNER, Famulus to Faustus
LISA, Maidservant to Faustus
JOHN FAUSTUS, a Conjurer
MEPHISTOPHELES, an Evil Spirit
A CARDINAL
A PRIEST
THE POPE
HELEN OF TROY, a Magical Apparition
JOHN FAUSTUS, in the body of his transformation
AZRAEL, Angel of the souls of the dead
THE EMPEROR
THE EMPRESS
A CHANCELLOR
A SECRETARY OF STATE
THE SOUL OF JOHN FAUSTUS
THE JUDGE
Devils, Citizens, Courtiers, Ladies, etc.

SCENES
I—Wittenberg: Faustus' Study, 1502
II—Rome: The Forum, 1503
III—Innsbruck: The Emperor's Court, 1527
IV—The Court of Heaven: Eternity

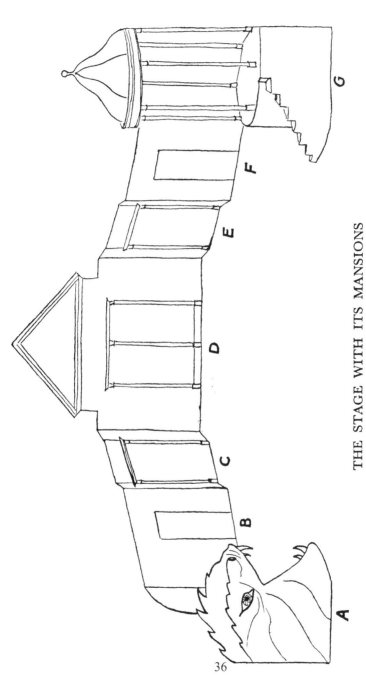

THE STAGE WITH ITS MANSIONS

A. Hell-mouth   B. Entrance right   C. Mansion 1   D. Mansion 2   E. Mansion 3   F. Entrance left   G. Heaven

SCENE I (*Mansion* 1)

WITTENBERG—FAUSTUS' STUDY

[*Lighted candles right and left in sconces. Centre, tall mirror covering entrance to Mansion 2. Left, big chart hung on rollers, showing eclipse of the sun. Right back, between Mansions 1 and 2, trick shelf with bottles, etc. On right wall, stoup of Holy Water. Left centre, chair, and table with books, parchments, flasks and other alchemical and astrological apparatus, together with a wax taper. On floor, down centre, a double circle and pentacle in white chalk. Enter from Mansion 1, WAGNER, carrying a lighted lantern, a long sword, a glass jar, five small lamps tied together, a cabbage and a dried stockfish, and reading a large book by the light of the lantern.*

WAGNER

Oh, dear ! Oh, dear ! I shall never be ready in time. Lisa ! Lisa ! (*shuffling to table*). So much to do since my master gave up theology and took to astrology and physic. " Ioth, Aglanabroth, El, Aniel, Anathiel, Anazim "— what terrible great hard words ! (*Sets down lantern, dropping cabbage.*) Alas ! what's that ? Oh, it's only the cabbage. (*Grovels for it, dropping sword.*) Heaven be praised ! I thought it was the precious Holy Water. (*Stands clutching all his parcels and holding book close to lantern.*) " Craton, Muriton, Agarion, Pentessaron "—Bless me ! I have forgotten the mandrakes—no, I remember, I put them in my pocket. (*Attempts to verify the mandrakes, dropping stockfish.*) Lisa !

[*Enter LISA, left.*

LISA

Oh, my poor Wagner ! How dreadfully burdened you are. Here, let me take some of those things. (*Picking up stockfish.*) What's this for ? Friday's dinner ?

37

WAGNER

It's a present from the poor fishmonger whose horoscope we cast free of charge. And this cabbage is from the old peasant we cured of the itch. I do hope I've got everything.

LISA (*putting fish and cabbage in her apron*)
I'm sure you have quite enough.

WAGNER

This is a flask of Holy Water from the River Jordan itself. Set it on the shelf. Carefully. It has been blessed by the Pope. And you must take these lamps and fill them with the very best consecrated oil. I'll put the Doctor's sword over here.

[*Wanders away, still clutching book, and leans sword against wall, right.*

LISA (*setting flask on shelf*)
Were there many at his lecture to-night ?

WAGNER

Yes, a great many. But I'm sure the most part of them care nothing for the brave things he tells them about Gemini and Capricorn and the movements of the planets. They only want to learn how to get rich, or to beg him to cure their diseases. There was a whole rag-tag and bob-tail besieging him at the door. In his place I wouldn't be troubled with them.

LISA

He is so kind. He will always help them if he can. He can't bear to see any one suffer (*at table, collecting lamps*).

WAGNER

So he sent me on ahead to prepare the room for him. We are to do great things to-night. Don't take the lantern. I need it to study my book.

LISA

But all the candles are lit.

WAGNER (*astonished*)

So they are ! I didn't notice. (*Importantly.*) But then, I'm so very busy. Now where in the world did I put the chalk ? I'm sure I had a piece somewhere.

LISA

I expect it's in your pocket.

WAGNER

I believe you're right. What a clever girl you are, Lisa, and so very, very pretty.

LISA

Foolish Wagner !

WAGNER

Don't you think you could call me Christopher ? (*Pleadingly.*) It isn't a bad name. Do please try. It would make me so happy. I'm very fond of you, Lisa.

LISA

Foolish Christopher (*skipping nimbly out of reach*). Now, you mustn't waste time. Find your chalk and get on with your work, or you won't be ready when Dr. Faustus comes.

WAGNER

The chalk ? Yes, I'm sure it's here, but it seems to be mixed up with something. (*Pulling bundle of roots from his pocket.*) Of course—the mandrakes. They must be hung in the chimney to dry.

LISA

What strange-looking things ! Put them in my apron. (*He tries to kiss her; she holds the lantern between them.*) Now, be a good Christopher and study your great book.

[*Exit, left, with lantern and lamps.*

WAGNER (*looking after her*)

Sometimes I think she doesn't take me seriously. Well, I must get on. (*Kneels and writes in circle, book in hand.*) The anagrams of God in the five points of the pentacle. IHS, El, Ya, Alpha, Omega. So. And the names of God between the points. Adonai. Emmanuel. Panthon. Tetragrammaton. Messias. So. And between the lamps in the circle, five signs of the Cross. One, two, three——

[*Re-enter* LISA, *with lamps.*

LISA

I have filled the lamps. What are you writing there?

WAGNER

Ah, that is a secret. Give them to me—so, one at each point of the star. These are high and mighty matters, and not for girls to know about. It's all written in this book, that was given to Dr. Faustus by the great conjurer, Cornelius Agrippa. To-morrow, we shall be richer and more powerful than the Emperor. We shall have spirits to fetch and carry for us——

LISA

What? You will not . . . He doesn't mean to . . . Oh, Christopher! There will be no danger to Dr. Faustus?

WAGNER

Of course not. No danger can pass this circle. Besides, I shall be there to protect him. How brave it will be! We shall be masters of all the treasure in the world. We shall heal all the troubles of mankind with a wave of the wand. We shall prank ourselves in costly apparel, and you and I will be married, Lisa, and fly to the court of the Grand Cham on the back of a winged basilisk. Tell me, dear Lisa, tell me——

LISA

I hear the Doctor coming.

[*Enter* FAUSTUS, *Mansion* 1. *He wears a great cloak over his doctor's gown.* LISA *runs to greet him.*

Oh, sir! how late you are! And how wet! Give me your cloak. I'm sure you must be tired to death. Sit down and rest. I will have a fine hot supper ready for you in a moment.

FAUSTUS

Thanks, Lieschen, thanks. But I shall need no supper. I have work to do.

[*Takes off his cloak and doctor's cap.* LISA *hangs them up.*

LISA

No supper ! Why, you have eaten nothing all day.

FAUSTUS

My work must be done fasting. (*He sits on a chair.*) Bring me a bowl of water, and the robe, slippers and girdle you will find in my chamber. Is everything ready, Wagner ?

[*Exit* LISA, *left.*

WAGNER

Yes, sir. I have this moment finished the circle.

FAUSTUS

See that it is accurately drawn. One of your spelling mistakes, or a touch of your usual absent-mindedness, might land us both in a very queer place. (WAGNER, *alarmed, checks all his hieroglyphics again by the book.*) Oh, God, I am sick at heart. When I see how ill this world is governed, and all the wretchedness that men suffer, I would give my immortal soul to be done with it all.

WAGNER (*crossing himself*)

Heaven forbid. What a thing to say ! When you think how easily your immortal soul might go wriggling away through a gap in the circle, like a rabbit through a fence. Or my soul, for that matter.

[*He carefully touches up a point of the pentacle.*

FAUSTUS

Don't be alarmed. You will be safe enough if you stay where I put you and don't lose your head and run away.

41

[*Re-enter* LISA *with slippers, bowl and napkin. She puts the bowl on the floor while she removes* FAUSTUS' *shoes and puts on his slippers.*

That will do. Leave it to me. I see you have drawn out the figure of the sun's eclipse.

WAGNER

Yes, sir. But I don't altogether understand it. The moon gives light to the earth. Why then do we see her black ?

FAUSTUS

The moon has no light of herself. When she passes between the earth and the sun she shows but as a mass of dark matter, as your head does, between me and that candle.

[*He washes his hands in the bowl* LISA *holds for him.*

WAGNER

I see. And if the sun were to pass between us and the moon, would he show dark also ?

FAUSTUS

No ; for he is the very source of the light, and in him is no darkness at all. My robe and girdle, Lieschen.

LISA

Oh, sir ! I don't like the look of that robe, and the girdle with all the strange words upon it. They are too much like what you have there upon the floor. I am afraid of them. Will you not sit and have your supper like a Christian, and leave these fearful conjuring tricks to ignorant, unhappy men who know no better ?

FAUSTUS

What is all this ? Have you been talking, Wagner ?

LISA

What do you need with riches and power and the court of the Grand Cham, and wicked spirits and basilisks—you that are happy in your great wisdom and learning ?

Child, the greater the wisdom, the greater the sorrow. The end of all our knowledge is to learn how helpless we are. Divinity, philosophy, astrology—I have studied them all. There are no springs of comfort in that barren desert of doctrine. Physic but lays a patch to the old garment; the stuff itself is rotten, warp and woof; the corruption eats deeper than our drugs can reach. (*Violently.*) What is this folly about riches and worldly delights? Do you think I care for such toys? But if magical power can aid me to resolve the mystery of wickedness, lay bare the putrefying sore at the heart of creation, break and remake the pattern of the inexorable stars—— I have frightened you. Fetch me my robe, and do not meddle with what you cannot understand. There, I know you mean well, but do not vex me now.

[*Exit* LISA, *left, removing bowl and shoes.*

Wagner, why do you not attend to your work, instead of chattering to Lisa?

[*Takes off his gown and lays it on the chair.*

WAGNER (*hurt*)

I have worked very hard indeed. I have purchased the lamps, ordered the oil, taken your sword to be ground, brought home the Jordan water, finished the circle and learnt a great many very long and difficult names out of this book. I hoped you would be pleased with me.

[*Re-enter* LISA *with robe and girdle and puts them on* FAUSTUS.

FAUSTUS

Why, so I am. You are an honest, industrious fellow—and if your heart is a better organ than your head, it was not you that had the making of them. Thank you, child. Now run away, and never trouble your pretty head about us. And remember, no matter what you may hear, you must not cross the threshold of this room to-night. On no pretence whatsoever. Do you hear me?

Yes, sir. May God and His holy angels protect us all.

[*Exit, left, taking* FAUSTUS' *gown.*

FAUSTUS

Now, Wagner, to work ! Bring the book to me.

WAGNER (*bringing stoup across from wall and giving
it to* FAUSTUS)

This is empty. Will you have the blessed water from the
Jordan ?

[*He lays the book on the table.*

FAUSTUS

Yes. But make haste; for this spirit will not come save
he be called between the ninth hour and midnight.

[WAGNER *brings flask and fills the stoup which* FAUSTUS *holds.*

FAUSTUS (*signing the water*)

In nomine Patris et Filii et Spiritus Sancti, exorcizo te,
creatura aquae, ut fias aqua exorcizata ad effugandam
omnem potestatem inimici. Amen.

WAGNER

Amen.

[*While* WAGNER *puts back the flask and changes it by means
of the trick shelf,* FAUSTUS *sprinkles the water within the circle.*

FAUSTUS

Asperges me Domine hyssopo et mundabor, lavabis me
et supra nivem dealbabor. Gloria Patri et Filio et Spiritui
Sancto.

WAGNER

Sicut erat in principio et nunc et semper et in saecula
saeculorum. Amen. (*He puts back the stoup and now brings the
sword, naked, to* FAUSTUS, *who has meanwhile taken the book
from the table and opened it.*) Must I put out the lights,
Master ?

FAUSTUS (*examining the circle*)
Put them all out, and bring me a lighted taper.

WAGNER (*takes taper from table, lights it at one of
the candles, and then extinguishes the lights*)
Oh, master, it's going to be very dark and not at all
comfortable. I don't think I care very much about being
rich and powerful and riding on b-b-basilisks. D-d-don't
you think it would be better to stop all this, and have
a nice little astrology lesson or something?

FAUSTUS
Take courage, Wagner. Thou wilt not desert me now?
There must be some meaning in this tormented universe,
where light and darkness, good and evil forever wrestle at
odds; and though God be silent or return but a riddling
answer, there are spirits that can be compelled to speak.
    [WAGNER *returns, carrying the taper.*
Now follow me into the circle, and see that thou close it
well after we have passed over.
    [*They step into the circle through a gap left in the figure, which*
WAGNER *closes carefully with chalk.*
Light the lamps.

WAGNER
My hand trembles. (*He lights the lamps.*) Oh, dear! what
will become of us? Ugh! Something brushed past my
face, like a bat. Would I were well out of this.
    [*He extinguishes the taper.*

FAUSTUS
Be silent. Stand back to back with me and be sure you
let neither hand nor foot stray beyond the circle. Now
we begin.
In the name of the most high God, maker of Heaven and
earth and of all things under the earth, Ioth, Aglanabroth,
El, Abiel, Anathiel, Amazim, Messias, Tolimi, Ischiros,

45

Athanatos, I require of Thee, O Lord, by the seal of Solomon and by the ineffable name wherewith he did bind the devils and shut them up, Adonai, Aglai, Tetragrammaton, grant me Thy virtue and power, to cite before me Thy spirits which were thrown down from Heaven, and in especial that spirit which is called Mephistopheles, that he may come and speak with me, and dispatch again at my command, without hurt to my body, soul and goods, and diligently fulfil the will of me Thy exorcist. Fiat, fiat, fiat. Amen.

[*Thunder.*

[*Here* FAUSTUS *may hand the book to* WAGNER *unnoticed, and so be relieved of it.*

I conjure thee, Mephistopheles, by the unspeakable name of God, and by His virtue and power, and by Him that harrowed Hell; I conjure and exorcise thee, by angels and archangels, by thrones, dominations, principalities and powers, by virtues, by cherubim and seraphim, and by the name of thy master, Lucifer, Prince of the East, that thou do come to us, here visibly before this circle, and that thou do make answer truly, without craft or deceit, unto all my demands and questions.

[*Thunder again, and Hell-mouth opens with a great noise and a red light.*

In the name of Him that liveth and reigneth for ever, and hath the keys of hell and of death, come hither to me, Mephistopheles.

[*Enter* MEPHISTOPHELES, *out of Hell, in the form of a lion with the tail of a serpent and the feet of a bull.*

WAGNER (*looking round over* FAUSTUS' *shoulder*)
Oh, help ! help ! Heaven defend us ! We are lost ! We're undone. (*He springs out of the circle and runs off, left. Flame and an explosion drive him back. A peal of diabolical laughter is heard.*) Mercy ! Help ! what shall I do ?

46

FAUSTUS

Spirit, I charge thee, hurt him not.

MEPHISTOPHELES

Enough. Let him go. Away with thee, mannikin ! Thy master and I have business together.

[WAGNER *runs out.*

FAUSTUS

And thou, Mephistopheles, put off this ugly shape, fit only to frighten children. Stand before me in the semblance of a man.

MEPHISTOPHELES

With pleasure. Nothing easier. (*He takes off his lion's head and tosses it negligently into Hell-mouth.*) And now, sir, what can I do for you, to justify the expenditure of so many big words and this great exhibition of fi-fo-fum ?

FAUSTUS

Answer me truly first concerning thyself. What art thou ?

MEPHISTOPHELES

Truly, you should know best, since you called me by name. But indeed, I am not particular. I will answer to anything you like to call me, for my name is legion, and Evil is one of my names.

FAUSTUS

Tell me, then, thou Evil, who made thee ?

MEPHISTOPHELES

He that made all things.

FAUSTUS

What ? did God make thee ? Was all the evil in the world made by God ? Beware what thou sayest; I know thee for a false and lying spirit.

MEPHISTOPHELES

That is a most unjust accusation. What lies have I ever told ? There is no need for lying, seeing that mankind are such fools.

47

How so ?

MEPHISTOPHELES

Why, tell them the truth and they will mislead themselves
by their own vanities and save me the trouble of invention.
I sat by Eve's shoulder in the shadow of the forbidden
tree. " Eat," said I, " and you shall become like God."
She and her silly husband ate, and it was so. Where was
the lie ? Was it my fault if they persuaded themselves that
God was everything they hankered to be—all-good, all-
wise, all-powerful and possessed of everlasting happiness ?

FAUSTUS

Is not God all these things ?

MEPHISTOPHELES

Is He these things ? Look at the world He made, and ask
yourself, what is He like that made it ? Would you not say
it was the work of a mad brain, cruel and blind and stupid
—this world where the thorn chokes the flower, where the
fox slays the fowl and the kite the fox, where the cat tor-
ments the mouse for pastime before she kills it for sport ?
Where men, made truly enough in the image of their
Maker, rend, ravish and torture one another, lay waste
the earth, burn up provinces for a title or a handful of
dirty metal, persecute for a pater-noster, and send a fellow-
fool to the rack for the shape of his nose or the name of
his mother's father ? War, fire, famine, pestilence—is He
all-good that delights in these, or all-powerful that likes
them not and endures them ? Ask thyself this.

FAUSTUS

I have asked it a hundred times without thy prompting.
It is as though my own heart spoke to me. Man's cruelty
is an abomination—but how can one justify the cruelty
of God ?

MEPHISTOPHELES

Is He all-wise, that had not the wits to keep out of the mess He had made, but must needs meddle with this business of being a man, and so left matters worse than He found them ? Why, He could not even speak His mind plainly, but all He said was so fumblingly expressed, men have been by the ears ever since, trying to make out His meaning. And was not that a prime piece of folly, to show up His nature thus—base and ignorant as any carpenter's son, too poor in spirit to argue in His own defence, too feeble to save His own skin from the hangman ? Everlasting happiness ? What happiness do you find in the history of the Man of Sorrows ? By their fruits ye shall know them.

FAUSTUS

It was He that said that.

MEPHISTOPHELES

So He did, in one of His more unguarded moments.

FAUSTUS

And yet, Mephistopheles, His very name has power to conjure thee from the bowels of hell.

MEPHISTOPHELES (*with an almost imperceptible hesitation*)

The power is not in the name. That name is powerful only because you believe in its power. Believe in your own power, and you can command me without any tricks of conjuration.

FAUSTUS

Wilt thou then come when I call ? Wilt thou stay with me and be my servant, and do and bring me all things whatsoever I shall desire ?

MEPHISTOPHELES

I shall always be with you, John Faustus. You have only to think upon me, and I shall be there.

FAUSTUS

And do my bidding?

MEPHISTOPHELES

With all my power.

FAUSTUS

Not harming me in any manner?

MEPHISTOPHELES

You need have no more fear of me than of yourself.

FAUSTUS

Come hither to me then, and shake hands upon the compact.

MEPHISTOPHELES

By all means—if you will first come out of the circle.

FAUSTUS

How can the circle hold thee back, since it has no power but by me, and I say, Come!

MEPHISTOPHELES (*again embarrassed*)

Very well argued. But the fact is, you and your servant have so drowned the place with Jordan water that I don't care about it. I am very susceptible to chills, and I should infallibly get cramp in my hoofs. Besides, my Master Lucifer forbids me to enter the circle.

FAUSTUS

And wherefore?

MEPHISTOPHELES

For the better encouragement of superstition. But come—command me something. A few sacks of gold, perhaps, or a little supper. You must be famished with all this nonsense of prayer and fasting.

FAUSTUS

Well, then, bring me food.

50

MEPHISTOPHELES

Ho, there, my merry devils. Food and wine for your master. Music, ho !

[*Music. Enter, right and left,* DEVILS *dancing, with platters of fruit, etc., and one with a goblet of wine, which they present to* FAUSTUS.

Drink, master, drink ! What ! Does the cursed fruit of the tree stick in thy throat still ? Drink, and drown that devil's gift of knowledge, from whence spring all the cares that afflict mankind. Drink—for the kingdom, the power and the glory are within thy grasp. Only stretch out thy hand and fear not.

FAUSTUS

Spirit, I fear thee not. Give me the cup.

MEPHISTOPHELES

First sheathe that sword; my delicate devils wince
Like women to see cold iron.

FAUSTUS (*sheathing his sword*)
Give me the cup.

[*As* FAUSTUS *stretches his hand beyond the protection,* MEPHISTOPHELES *catches him by the wrist and pulls him out of the circle. Thunder; and all the lamps are immediately extinguished.*

If God's so harsh a stepfather to His sons
Then must we turn adventurers, and carve out
Our own road to salvation. Here's to change ! (*Drinks.*)
O the wine's brave; it dances in the blood
And whirls in the brain, glowing and giving life
As though the vintagers had put in prison
The very sun, and pressed him with the grapes
Till all the vats ran fire.

MEPHISTOPHELES (*aside*)
And so it should,
Seeing what cellars it came from.

CP   51

FAUSTUS

                God's old realm,
Like an estate farmed by a bankrupt, dwindles
The sluggard way to ruin; her rank hedgerows
Drop down their brambles over the sour ditch;
Bindweed, tough tares, and tangling restharrow choke
Her furrows, where the plough stands idle, rust
Reddening the share; and in her hungry fields
Only the blind mole and the skipping coney
Drive their dark tunnels 'twixt the thistle and thorn.
We'll starve at home no longer. The soul's a world,
And hath her hemispheres, as the world hath,
Where thoughts put forth like galleons, leaving behind
These weedgrown crumbling harbours shoaled with time,
To sail new seas, steer by strange stars, cross over
Unknown meridians, and by pathless coasts
Explore her dusky Indias.

MEPHISTOPHELES

                Well, well, well—
I have heard young men speak thus.

FAUSTUS

                Young men speak thus?
I am not old, Mephistopheles. I have grown
A little grey, perhaps, with study and labour,
But I'm not old at all.

MEPHISTOPHELES

                Go to, go to.
[*He leads* FAUSTUS *to the mirror.*
You are older than you should be. Mark you, mark
How lean men grow who try to save the world.
That line betwixt the brows—what wrote it there
But squinnying close at books, and frowning down
Your nose at ignorance? And the sour folds
At the corner of the mouth, the virtuous stamp
That Pharisees wear like phylacteries,

Proclaiming at what dear and grudged expense
They are chaste and sober; and the red-rimmed eyes
That weep to see how men enjoy their lusts,
Being so strangely happier than the godly.

FAUSTUS
I have wept for the woes of men, fighting like beasts,
Tortured like helpless beasts.

MEPHISTOPHELES
      Let that alone,
The remedy makes it worse. Beast wars with beast
And slays and leaves no rancour. Heartbreak comes
With man's self-consciousness and righteous hate,
When one ferocious virtue meets another
As quarrelsome as itself, good savaging good
Like so many angry lobsters in a basket
Pinching each other's claws off. Now, behold
What you now are, and what you might have been
In the innocent world, if man had never meddled
With virtue and the dismal knowledge of God.

[*The image of* FAUSTUS *fades from the mirror and the image
of the* YOUNG FAUSTUS *takes its place. It mimics* FAUSTUS.

FAUSTUS
Is that myself, or the young fair Apollo
Stepped from his golden chariot and new bathed
In springs of Thessaly? It moves like me
And its lips mimic mine with silent speech.
Can it be I indeed?

[*As he turns to question* MEPHISTOPHELES *the image of*
HELEN *appears in the mirror behind the image of* FAUSTUS *in
the place where* MEPHISTOPHELES *stands behind the real*
FAUSTUS.

MEPHISTOPHELES
Look then again.
53

FAUSTUS

O wonder of the world! O soul! O beauty
Beyond all splendour of stars!

[*As* FAUSTUS *moves towards the mirror,* MEPHISTOPHELES
moves to intercept him, and at the same time the image of HELEN
moves, so that as the image of FAUSTUS *clasps* HELEN, FAUSTUS
finds himself clutching MEPHISTOPHELES.

Hence! Let me pass!

[*He breaks from* MEPHISTOPHELES. *As he touches the mirror,
the vision vanishes. Thunder again.*

Hell and confusion! Damned, damned juggling tricks,
Nothing but sorcery!

MEPHISTOPHELES

What did you expect
When you called *me* up?

FAUSTUS

Bring her to me again
In the living flesh.

MEPHISTOPHELES

Fool, she is not for you
Nor any man. Illusion, all illusion!
For this is Grecian Helen, hell-born, hell-named,
Hell in the cities, hell in the ships, and hell
In the heart of man, seeking he knows not what.
You are too careful of your precious soul
To lay fast hold on Helen. She is mirage
Thrown on the sky by a hot reality
Far below your horizon.

FAUSTUS

Can you not bring me
Where Helen is?

MEPHISTOPHELES

I might—but at a cost
You might not wish to pay. In any case
Not as you are. If you would play the lover

54

You must look the part. Throw off this foolish weed !
Lights there !

[*The candles are lit of their own accord.*

Bring forth apparel for your master,
Faustus the conjurer, Faustus the magician,
Faustus the master of the words of power,
Prince of the prince of the air !

[DEVILS *enter and take* FAUSTUS' *robe and apparel him richly.*

And bring him gold
To fill his purse. He must live delicately.

[*Gold brought in a shining dish.*

All the lost treasure of the world is ours,
That men have sweated, toiled, fought, died to gain,
And wasted—the pirate's and the gambler's spoil,
The miser's hoard, the harlot's wage, the grudged
Profits of usury, the assassin's fee,
The politician's bribe, the nation's wealth
Blown from the belching cannon—all flow down
Through veins and vessels of their native earth
In one red stream to the hot heart of hell,
Gushing and hissing—listen !

[*Appropriate noises from Hell-mouth.*

The roar of the furnace !
Hark how the anvils clang in that black stithy
To the hammer-strokes forging the chains of gold
For the neck of the world, bars, ingots, cataracts
Of ringing coin ! Power, power, for thy bold hand—
Take it and use it !

VOICE (*without, right*)
Alms, for the love of God,
For sweet St. Charity, pity the poor blind.

[FAUSTUS *stands arrested, with the gold in his hands.*

MEPHISTOPHELES
That is what God allows; will you allow it ?

55

FAUSTUS

No, by the powers of Hell ! If God permits
Such suffering in this damnable world, He's blind,
Deaf, mad, cruel, helpless, imbecile or dead !

[*He rushes to entrance, Mansion* i.

Look, here is gold—gold to thy heart's desire—
No man shall want, if Faustus can prevent it.

[*He flings money out to the beggar. Cries without.*

MEPHISTOPHELES (*at Hell-mouth*)

Lucifer, Lucifer ! the bird is caught—
You may turn off the lights and put the cat out
And shut the door and go downstairs to bed.
I shall not be home for supper.

[*Laughter. Hell-mouth closes. Re-enter* FAUSTUS.

These virtuous fools !

FAUSTUS

O, power is grateful to the heart—to change
Sorrow to happiness in a twinkling—blot
The word " Despair " out of life's lexicon,
And make joy blossom in the desert sand.
Bring me swift horses—bring me the wings of the wind !
We'll fly to the wide world's four distracted corners
Like a great gust of laughter, scattering delight.
We'll do—what will we not do, Mephistopheles ?
We will forget old sins—we'll break the cross,
Tear the usurper Christ from His dark throne
And this time bury Him deep and well, beyond
All hope of resurrection.

[*Knocking at entrance, left.*

Hush ! who's there ?

WAGNER (*without*)

O master, dear master, how is it with you ? If you are not
carried off body and bones into Hell, speak to me !

56

FAUSTUS

All's well, Wagner. Wait. I will let thee in presently. Listen, Mephistopheles. You must stay with me, be known as my servant, show yourself only in your human shape, and not alarm my household too much.

MEPHISTOPHELES

I am entirely at your service.

FAUSTUS

Here, take my cloak. (*He puts his cloak on* MEPHISTOPHELES.) Try to look a little more respectable. You would be more convincing in a stout pair of boots.

MEPHISTOPHELES

I will procure boots immediately.

FAUSTUS

And hark'ee. See that you offer no offence to Lieschen. She is a good, modest, virtuous child.

MEPHISTOPHELES

Set your mind at rest. On such as her I have no power.

FAUSTUS

And be gentle with my poor Wagner. So. I will open the door. (*Crossing left, he turns and adds in a fierce whisper.*) Tuck your tail up ! (*At entrance.*) Come in, Wagner.

[*Enter* WAGNER.

WAGNER

O Doctor, Doctor, praise God you're safe and sound. Lisa and I have been so frightened. Such dreadful noises —and the thunder—the whole house shook. We've been saying our prayers in the kitchen. Do forgive me for being so foolish and cowardly. I thought you were killed and the devil had eaten you, so I came to see if I could do anything. Has the devil gone away ? The room smells shockingly of sulphur.

FAUSTUS

There's nobody here but this—gentleman, whom I have engaged to be my personal attendant.

WAGNER (*to* MEPHISTOPHELES)

How do you do, sir ? God be with you. (*Calling off.*) It's all right, Lisa. The devil's gone. (*To* MEPHISTOPHELES.) What a dreadful night to arrive in. Are you wet ? Perhaps you would like to change your shoes ? I could lend you slippers. It's so unwise to sit in damp feet. What size do you . . . ? Oh, I beg your pardon (*to* FAUSTUS). How thoughtless of me. I didn't notice the poor creature was so afflicted.

FAUSTUS

You are too officious.

MEPHISTOPHELES (*to* WAGNER)

It's very kind of you, but I came—by the underground way.

WAGNER

I see. Well (*anxious to do something*), the room is very untidy. Shall I help you off with your robe, Doctor ? Dear me, it's off already. What a fine suit of clothes you have got !

VOICES (*without*)

Help ! help ! . . . Hand over the money ! . . . Thieves ! Murder ! . . . Strike him down . . . Give me the gold . . . Ah ! would you ! . . . Down with you ! (*Noise of fighting.*)

LISA (*off*)

Help, watchman, help ! Watch ! Watch !

FAUSTUS

What is all that ?

MEPHISTOPHELES

The effects of your benevolence, I fancy.

[*Enter* LISA, *left.*

58

LISA

Alas ! alas ! Here's a poor old blind man been set upon and robbed under our windows and a whole crowd of ruffians quarrelling for the money. I saw three men stabbed. (*Noise increases.*) Oh, mercy.

FAUSTUS

Are men mad to abuse the gifts we give them ? (*He rushes off, Mansion* 1, *drawing his sword as he goes.*) What is God about ?

WAGNER

I don't understand all this.

MEPHISTOPHELES (*primly*)

Indiscriminate charity is a device of the devil.

LISA (*with a little shriek*)

Oh, Wagner, who's that ?

MEPHISTOPHELES

The Doctor's servant, so please you.

LISA (*recoiling against* WAGNER)

I don't like him. I'm afraid of him. Who is he ?

WAGNER

Bless me, Lisa, where are your manners ? (LISA *drops* MEPHISTOPHELES *a reluctant curtsey and escapes, left.*) You must excuse her. We have all been upset by the thunderstorm. (*With holy-water stoup.*) Oh, dear, this is empty again. (*He hands it to* MEPHISTOPHELES.) Do you mind holding it while I fill it up ?

[*Goes up to shelf, back.*

MEPHISTOPHELES

Pray don't apologise. Women have their fancies. I get along very well with them as a rule, but every so often, the nicest girls will take a positive dislike to me. I've no idea why.

WAGNER (*returning with flask*)
Very strange—but as you say, girls are quite unaccountable. Please hold it carefully. This is very special Holy Water from the——

[*Re-enter* FAUSTUS, *Mansion* 1.

FAUSTUS

The watch have arrested them all—Wagner ! leave that alone !

[*He is too late. The water steams up and bubbles over the bowl, which* MEPHISTOPHELES *lets fall.*

WAGNER (*crossing himself*)
Holy Mary ! Heaven deliver us ! Oh, sir, sir ; I fear me you are gotten into very ill company.

MEPHISTOPHELES

So that cat's out of the bag !

FAUSTUS

What will you do, Wagner ? Will you quit my service ?

WAGNER

No, Doctor, no. I'll not leave you alone to face danger again. I'm sorry for what I did. But from henceforth I'll be as brave as a lion.

FAUSTUS

Thanks, my faithful Wagner.

MEPHISTOPHELES (*clapping* WAGNER *on the back*)
Why, that's a bold fellow, to be ready to live cheek by jowl with the devil.

WAGNER

Why, so must every Christian man. And the devil we see is less terrible than the devil we don't see (*shaking* MEPHISTOPHELES *off*). But there's no need to be familiar. (*To* FAUSTUS.) And what happens next, if you please ?

FAUSTUS

We're off to Rome, to beard God in His own stronghold.

WAGNER (*stolidly*)

Are you going by sea, or—underground ?

MEPHISTOPHELES

Through the air, my lad. By enchantment.

FAUSTUS

Those winged dragons you are always talking about.

WAGNER (*drily*)

Just as well. You were always a very poor sailor.

FAUSTUS

You and Lisa can do as you like. Come, Mephistopheles !

[*He goes out, right.*

WAGNER (*going off, left*)

Poor Lisa ! She won't like this very much. (*Turning suddenly.*) Here, you ! Clear up all this mess. And look sharp. I'm going to pack.

[*Exit.*

MEPHISTOPHELES (*staring after him*)

Well, I'll be—blessed !

[*He claps his hands. Music, and enter four* DEVILS, *who clear the stage.* MEPHISTOPHELES *goes out by the same way as* FAUSTUS.

SCENE II (*Mansion* 3)

ROME—THE FORUM

[*Enter from Mansion* 1 (*Wittenberg*) WAGNER *and* LISA *in travelling dress, with luggage. They walk all about the stage and come at last to Rome* (*Mansion* 3).

WAGNER

Here we are at last—safely in Rome ! It has been a long journey from Wittenberg.

LISA

Long and wearisome ! I'm so grateful to you, kind Wagner, for coming with me, instead of flying away on the winged dragon with Dr. Faustus and—that other, terrible man.

WAGNER

I shouldn't dream of letting you travel unprotected. Besides, I have thought it all over and decided that winged dragons are all right for learned philosophers, but plain folk like you and me do best on the beaten track. (*Looking about him.*) What a fine city Rome is, to be sure ! A hundred times bigger than Wittenberg.

LISA

How shall we ever find the Doctor out, in this great labyrinth of streets and houses ?

WAGNER

We shall find him, never fear. During all these months he will certainly have become very great and famous. This wide square must be the market-place. Let's sit down here and rest, and presently we will ask some passer-by to direct us to the Doctor's lodging.

[*They sit down, left. Enter, from Mansion* 3, *a* CARDINAL *and a* PRIEST *conversing; they come down centre.*

CARDINAL

If such be the case, then His Holiness should be told about it. And in the meantime, by all means speak to the people.

PRIEST

I assure Your Eminence, it is as I say. The whole city is disturbed by the miracles of Dr. Faustus.

WAGNER (*to* LISA)

There ! what did I tell you ?

CARDINAL

Where does he come from ?

PRIEST

From Wittenberg, they say, some twelve months since. His learning is undoubtedly great and his wealth unlimited ; though how he came by them, God or the devil knows. He distributes gold to all and sundry, heals the sick, raises the dead, and corrupts the minds of the poor by his vile, atheistical talk. The churches are deserted. Sundays and week-days, the people throng to the lectures of Dr. Faustus.

LISA (*approaching them*)

O Father ! If you know Dr. Faustus, pray tell me where he is to be found.

PRIEST

What ! Is this another of them ? Away, shameless girl.

CARDINAL

The less you have to do with John Faustus the better. His life is scandalous, his followers godless—

PRIEST

Heretical—

CARDINAL

Idolaters—

PRIEST

Sorcerers—

CARDINAL

Whoremongers—

PRIEST

Devil-worshippers—

CARDINAL

Apostate—

PRIEST

Excommunicate—

CARDINAL

And irretrievably damned !

LISA

No, no ! if you knew him you would not say such things. He is good and kind.

WAGNER

The most learned man in Christendom.

PRIEST

He is the open enemy of God and Holy Church.

CARDINAL

And known to be in league with the devil. (*As* WAGNER *winces at this home-thrust.*) Will you deny it ?

LISA

Alas !

WAGNER (*stoutly*)

If Dr. Faustus commands the spirits it is to a good and pious end. He is very clever, and knows how to bind the devil to the service of God.

CARDINAL

You are sadly deceived. It is forbidden to cast out devils by Beelzebub. Nor will a good end justify such vile and wicked means.

WAGNER (*drawing* LISA *away*)
Come away, Lisa. They are jealous of him. We will ask somebody else.

PRIEST (*pulling* CARDINAL *across, right*)
Besides, Eminence, the end he seeks is very dangerous.

[*Various* TOWNSFOLK *begin to drift in, Mansion 3 and left.* MEPHISTOPHELES *enters and stands, right, showing in pantomime that he overhears the conversation of* CARDINAL *and* PRIEST.

He preaches everywhere that he can abolish pain and suffering from the world. And what, pray, would become of religion, if there were no such thing as suffering?

CARDINAL
What, indeed? Who would repent of sin, if he did not fear to suffer in this world? Or if pain and sickness were not there, to put him in mind of his latter end?

PRIEST
Nobody would go to confession, or pay for masses, or indulgences, or prayers for the sick. There would be no pilgrimages, no alms-giving, no thank-offerings, no rich bequests to the Church. And what would happen to us, I should like to know? No sin, no sermon; no cross, no cardinal; no pain, no Pope!

[MEPHISTOPHELES *withdraws again.*

CARDINAL
Quite so; but I should not stress that point in your address. Begin now. I will go and acquaint His Holiness with all this.

[PRIEST *mounts the rostrum, left.*

Give ear, good people. The reverend father has somewhat to say to you.

[*Exit* CARDINAL, *Mansion 3.* FAUSTUS *and* MEPHISTOPHELES *enter unnoticed at back of* CROWD, *who gather right.*

65

PRIEST

Citizens of Rome ! Sons and daughters of Holy Church ! It has come to the ears of His Holiness the Pope that many among you are led away by the abominable doctrines of one John Faustus—(*cheers for* FAUSTUS)—a charlatan, a sorcerer, a man of lewd and evil life (*cries of dissent*) who would delude you by the promise to do away with toil and labour, with poverty, pain and suffering, and ensure to every man health, wealth and long days upon the earth. (*Renewed cheers.*) Alas, my children, why will you be deceived ? Do you not know that toil and suffering were ordained by God for the sins of Adam ? And that only by suffering are you made worthy to enter into the joys of Heaven ? Do you think there is any way to salvation, except by the cross whereon our Saviour suffered for the sins of all ? (*Murmurs of doubt.*) All of you will come to die some day—and how will you answer then for a life spent in sloth and luxury ? Will it be easy, think you, to put off that proud and stubborn flesh that no suffering has mortified, no sorrow subdued ? Let not the lust of gold corrupt you, for it is easier for a camel to pass through the eye of a needle than for a rich man to enter into the Kingdom of Heaven. Turn away your hearts from idols ; embrace the cross and repent ; return to the bosom of Holy Church, to whom alone it is given to bind and loose and free you from the domination of evil. If this fellow Faustus seeks to persuade you from your allegiance to the Church, it is that he may destroy your souls. He is a damned soul, burning in a hell of hatred, and would drag you all down along with him to damnation.

FAUSTUS (*leaping upon the rostrum, right*)

That is a lie !

PRIEST

Who dares to say so ?

FAUSTUS

I say so. I am John Faustus.

66

PRIEST

Silence, thou rascal !

FAUSTUS

I will not be silent. I tell you to your face that your Church is corrupt, your doctrine a lie and your God a cruel tyrant.

[*Murmurs among the crowd.* MEPHISTOPHELES *whispers in* FAUSTUS' *ear.*

PRIEST

Out of thine own mouth, atheist ! Do you hear this fellow blaspheme against God and His Holy Church ?

FAUSTUS

The Church ? Hark to the sly priest with his own axe to grind ! The Church is rich and you are poor. Her prelates go in rich robes, and you in stinking rags. Wherefore ? Ask him that preaches the money out of your pockets to keep him and his greasy brethren in idleness. He cares nothing for your souls, but only for the gold he can squeeze out of you.

PRIEST

It is false.

FAUSTUS

It is true. Ask my servant here, that heard him say as much to the Cardinal.

CROWD

Shame ! shame ! . . . Down with the idle priests !

FAUSTUS

Why should you slave to enrich these blood-suckers ?

CROWD (*rushing towards* PRIEST)

Blood-suckers ! . . . Horse-leeches ! . . . Down with the priests ! . . . Sack the monasteries ! . . . Come on ! . . . Sack ! slay ! . . . Away with them ! etc.

PRIEST

Beware ! Touch not God's anointed !

[CROWD *hesitates.*

Think, before you call down the terrible vengeance of Heaven. What saith the Scripture ? Thou shalt not suffer a witch to live. Faustus is a witch and a sorcerer, and his servant is the devil incarnate. By their fruits ye shall know them. They work the works of darkness, and their gifts shall bring, not blessings, but a curse. Is that not so ?

FIRST WOMAN

It is so. We were poor, and Faustus gave us gold. Now my husband has left his home and gone to live wantonly with harlots.

FIRST MAN

I was a cripple and lived by begging. Faustus cured me, and now I must work to live.

SECOND WOMAN

I was barren, and Faustus laid his spells upon me, and now I have borne a child that is possessed by seven devils.

SECOND MAN

I loved my wife, and she died. Faustus raised her from the dead and lo ! she is become a shrew, a vixen, the veriest termagant in Rome.

WIFE

Thou art a beast to say so. Take that, coward !

[*She beats her husband. Laughter and commotion.*

FAUSTUS

Ungrateful dogs !—

PRIEST

Hark, how he turns upon you now !

CROWD

Down with him ! . . . Sorcerer ! . . . Witch ! . . . Burn
him ! . . . Drown him ! . . . Tear him to pieces ! . . .
Witch ! Witch ! Witch !

[*A rush is made against* FAUSTUS.

FAUSTUS (*in a tone of command*)

Mephistopheles !

MEPHISTOPHELES

Back, little men ! (*The crowd is frozen into immobility.*) You
cannot move hand or foot to harm my master.

CROWD

What's this ? . . . I am paralysed . . . I am turned to stone
. . . I can't lift my arm . . . I can't put my foot down
. . . etc.

MEPHISTOPHELES

A nice lot of fools you look ! A most edifying regiment of
wax-works ! And Master Priest there, fixed on one foot,
like an image of Hermes in a garden-pool ! Pray, sir, are
you afflicted with a sudden cramp ? Why not take counsel
of Dr. Faustus, that is so eminent a physician ? Shall I
tickle them for you, master ? Shall I twist their bones ?
Shall I put fire under their tails ?

FAUSTUS

Enough ! release them, Mephistopheles.

[*The* CROWD *put down their arms and legs again and stand
rubbing themselves foolishly.*

O men, men ! Why will you quarrel and fight ? Why seek
to harm me, that have only loved you and laboured for
your good ? I would free you from the burden of fear and
pain and poverty that God has laid upon you. Listen to
me. If God made all things, He made the evil that tor-
ments you, and why should you serve so cruel a master ?
If He made not all things, He is not God, and you may
defy Him as I do. Be men ! Rouse yourselves ! Throw

off this bondage of superstition, and learn to know your friends from your foes. I am not your enemy. God is the enemy of us all——

[*Enter, Mansion* 3, *the* POPE, *carrying a crucifix in his hand, and with* CARDINAL *in attendance.*

POPE
Then learn to face the enemy. Speak on, my child.
I stand here for God.

CROWD (*falling to their knees*)
The Holy Father !

FAUSTUS
Stand, then, old man, and hear what I would spit
Into God's teeth, were we set face to face
Even in the Courts of Heaven. God's heart is evil,
Vengeful and tyrannous. He hates the flesh,
The sweet flesh that He made; He treads down beauty
In the winepress of His wrath, pashing it out
To the sour wine of sacrifice; His eye
Is jaundiced to behold such happiness
As men may snatch out of a tortured world.
Look on the symbol in thy hand—the sceptre
Thou rul'st with in His name—it is the yardstick,
The very measure of the devilish hatred
He bears to man, were man His very Son.
Men ! I stand here for man, and in man's name
    [*He springs upon the* POPE *and snatches the crucifix from him.*
Defy God's rule, break His accursed sceptre
And smite His regent down.
    [*He lifts the crucifix to slay the* POPE. *The* CROWD *exhibit horror, but are held back by* MEPHISTOPHELES.

WAGNER (*throwing himself between them*)
O master, master !

FAUSTUS (*flinging* WAGNER *off*)
You here ? Stand aside !
70

LISA (*catching* FAUSTUS *by the arm*)

Oh, Doctor, dear Doctor ! for shame ! What ! Strike an old man—helpless—unresisting ?

[FAUSTUS *pauses in some confusion.*

Oh, no ! how could you dream of it ? You will not. I know you will not. Not the devil himself could change your kind heart so. And you will not break the image of our dear Lord, who loved us so well and gave His life for us !

[*During this speech,* MEPHISTOPHELES *retreats and the* CROWD *closes threateningly in on* FAUSTUS.

FAUSTUS (*letting the crucifix drop into* WAGNER'S *hands*)
O Lisa, Lisa !

[*He looks about him, sees the menacing looks of the* CROWD *and goes on in an exhausted voice:*

I too love men; but they are all against me.
They hug their chains; the sacrificial iron
Cankers them at the core. I am not afraid
To suffer; for their sakes I would be damned
Willingly, so I first might do away
Suffering for ever from the pleasant earth.
And here stands power, like a smooth engine, ready
For good or ill alike. Being powerful,
I might be happy—might I not be happy ?—
But still the cry of the poor is in my ears
Intolerably. (*To the* POPE): You they call Holy Father—
A kind, compassionate title, " Holy Father "—
Will you be blind to truth ? God, having power,
Uses it like a devil; if He were good
He would turn back the ruthless wheel of time
To the golden age again. I am not God,
But can command the devil's power to serve
Good ends. Which is the devil—God, or I ?
Do you be judge between us.

71

POPE
                    O my poor child,
How much unhappiness is in store for thee !
For thou art taken in the toils of God,
That are more delicate than the spider's thread,
More strong than iron; and though thou wander far
As hell from Heaven, His cunning hand shall twitch
The line, and draw thee home. There is no rest
For such as thee, that bear upon their hearts
The brand of God, and, warring against God,
Make war upon themselves. Thou must be patient,
For God is very patient. Dost thou think
I cannot feel thy griefs ? I am the Pope,
Set on a tower above the plains of time
To watch how evil is at odds with good,
And to abide the issue, helpless, save
As prayer and wisdom and the grace of God
Shall give me strength. Hard it is, very hard,
To travel up the slow and stony road
To Calvary, to redeem mankind; far better
To make but one resplendent miracle,
Lean through the cloud, lift the right hand of power
And with a sudden lightning smite the world perfect.
Yet this was not God's way, Who had the power,
But set it by, choosing the cross, the thorn,
The sorrowful wounds. Something there is, perhaps,
That power destroys in passing, something supreme,
To whose great value in the eyes of God
That cross, that thorn, and those five wounds bear witness.
Son, go in peace; for thou hast sinned through love;
To such sin God is merciful. Not yet
Has thy familiar devil persuaded thee
To that last sin against the Holy Ghost
Which is, to call good evil, evil good.
Only for that is no forgiveness—Not
That God would not forgive all sins there are,

Being what He is; but that this sin destroys
The power to feel His pardon, so that damnation
Is consequence, not vengeance; and indeed
So all damnation is. I will pray for thee.
And you, my children, go home, gird your loins
And light your lamps, beseeching God to bring
His kingdom nearer, in what way He will.

[*Exeunt* POPE, CARDINAL *and* PRIEST, *Mansion* 3. CROWD *go out left and right. Manent* FAUSTUS, LISA, WAGNER *and* MEPHISTOPHELES.

MEPHISTOPHELES (*somersaulting across the stage and bowing derisively after the retreating* POPE)

Go in peace, old gentleman, go in peace ! Did ever a man use so many words to confess his own incompetence ? That fellow has no business in Peter's seat—he ought to be in Parliament. Come, Master—will you take the road to Calvary, and sup at the Skull-and-Crossbones ?

FAUSTUS

I am tired,. tired, Mephistopheles. Follow Christ ? That way is too long and too uncertain.

MEPHISTOPHELES

His way was folly and failure. I told you so, and now the Pope confirms it. Take your own way, in the devil's name, and shake a little sense into mankind.

FAUSTUS

My way frightens them. They have not even the heart to be grateful for my gifts.

WAGNER (*simply*)

Well, they are the devil's gifts after all. Perhaps it's true that they don't turn out very well. I'm sure people were very grateful in Wittenberg. Don't you remember ? All those presents of fish and vegetables ? I had hard work to carry them home.

LISA

Won't you come back to Wittenberg and heal the sick
with your drugs and simples as you did before ? Indeed,
indeed you were happier then.

FAUSTUS

Much happier, Lisa.

MEPHISTOPHELES

If you were happy, why did you send for me ?

WAGNER (*threatening* MEPHISTOPHELES *with the crucifix*)
Will you kindly go away and stop interfering.

[MEPHISTOPHELES *retreats.*

LISA

They are waiting for you, Doctor, and longing for your
return—all the poor and the sorrowful, and the mothers
with their sick children. They love you so much—we all
love you in Wittenberg.

FAUSTUS

Do they love me, Lisa ? Do you think that is happiness,
after all ? To take the easy way—to love and be beloved,
and not trouble to understand or get things altered ?
Perhaps. Every day the same sun rises, and year by year
the spring returns. Have the swallows built again under
the eaves of my window ?

LISA

Oh, yes ! Before we left home there were five speckled
eggs in the nest.

FAUSTUS

There is peace in those quiet streets, cool and deep
beneath the leaning gables. Let us go home, and find a
little love before we die. They love me in Wittenberg. . . .
Do you love me, Lisa ?

LISA

Alas ! I think I have loved you all my life.

WAGNER

Oh, God !

MEPHISTOPHELES

Didn't you know that ? Any fool could have seen it.

FAUSTUS

Poor child ! You should find a better lover. I am growing
old, Lisa. I have forgotten how to love.

WAGNER

I am a fool indeed. But that's nothing new.

LISA

You are the most wonderful man in all the world—far too
great and good for me.

FAUSTUS

Hush ! that is foolishness. But a very sweet foolishness.
Look at me. Your eyes are like quiet pools with the stars
reflected in them.

MEPHISTOPHELES

Cheer up, fool. I know how to deal with this.

WAGNER

I don't want any of your help.

MEPHISTOPHELES

But *she* does. Do you think he cares twopence for her ?

FAUSTUS

My head aches. I am homesick. Take me in your arms
and comfort me.

LISA

With all my heart.

MEPHISTOPHELES

Hush-a-bye, baby, on the tree-top ! Do you call this love ?

WAGNER

What else do you call it ?

MEPHISTOPHELES

Childishness. All men are fretful children when they can't get their own way. Love ? Fiddlesticks !

LISA

Does it ache much ?

FAUSTUS

Not now. There is rest in your presence, because there is rest in your soul.

MEPHISTOPHELES

Rest, indeed ? We'll see about that. Sacripant ! Belphegor !
    [*Calling off.*

FAUSTUS

What was that song you used to sing while the bread was a-baking ? All about Kings and Queens ?

LISA

That little, nursery song ?

MEPHISTOPHELES (*calling off*)

Here's a soul drowsing into Paradise. Whips ! Whips !

LISA (*sings*)
        Five silver fishes swimming in the sea,
        Five gold birds in a sycamore tree,
    [*Enter* HELEN, *right, with* DEVILS *attending her.*
        Five red deer running over the land,
        Five jewel-rings upon my hand.

MEPHISTOPHELES (*in the ear of* FAUSTUS)

Master, where are your eyes ?

FAUSTUS

Gadfly ! Let me sleep.

LISA (*sings*)
        When trees grow tall and leaves grow green
        You shall be king and I shall be queen.

MEPHISTOPHELES

Nay, dream on if you will. Sloth is a sin and serves my purpose; though there are merrier ways to be damned.

FAUSTUS (*freeing his eyes from* LISA'S *hand and sitting up*)
Away with you to hell. Be off, I say. (*He sees* HELEN.)
O my soul !

HELEN

John Faustus !

FAUSTUS (*leaping to his feet*)
Call me across a void of empty stars
And I shall hear.

HELEN
O love, hast thou forgotten ?

FAUSTUS

Not till the seas run dry; not till the centre
Kiss the circumference, and time's iron hand
Crack the great axle of the world asunder !
O Helen, Helen, Helen, I have loved thee
Before time was.

LISA
Come back, sweet love, come back !

WAGNER

Master, beware ! 'Tis witchcraft.

FAUSTUS
It is the voice
Of all the world's desire.

LISA
Oh, he is lost.

[*She falls into the arms of* WAGNER, *who helps her off.*

FAUSTUS

In what miraculous dream, in what far land,
Under what magic boughs, did thou and I
Lie once, and watch the sun shift through the leaves

Glinting the golden apples, when Troy town
Was yet unbuilt, that now is but a song
Almost beyond all memory ? When did we learn
Immortal love ? What unimagined page
Of scripture holds our legendary names,
Faustus and Helen ?

HELEN

My name is Helen now;
God's wrath, and ruin of distressful stars
Have made me so accurst. But once, ah, once
Adam lay on my breast and called me Lilith—
Long, long ago, in the old, innocent garden
Before Eve came, bringing her gift of knowledge
And shame where no shame was. The sons of Eve
Are all ashamed of me.

FAUSTUS

Are all athirst
For thee, thou star of more than mortal hope
To men !

HELEN

Shame and desire eat out their hearts,
For they are Adam's seed. And thou wast Adam,
Whose boyhood love was mine. So, when I call,
Thou canst not choose but turn to me again
From the very arms of Eve. Bone of thy bone
Is she, earth of the earth; she gives thee rest,
As the kind earth shall rest thy bones at last.
I am the fire in the heart, the plague eternal
Of vain regret for joys that are no more.

FAUSTUS

Wherefore no more ? I have returned to thee
Across the barren ways of world and time;
My soul is in thy breast. Take me to thee,
That we may love and laugh in innocence
With the everlasting gods ! Devils, stand back !

78

I will to Helen. In the tremendous name
Of power ineffable, by the seven-fold seal
Of Adonai, back !

[*The* DEVILS *restrain him still.*

What barrier's here
My witchcraft cannot break ?

HELEN

The bitter knowledge
Of good and evil. None may touch my lips
While on his own hangs still the fatal taste
Of Eve's sharp apple.

FAUSTUS

Paris had thy kiss.

HELEN

Paris cast back the apple to the gods,
Whose ringing discord jarred the towers of Troy
In ruin down.

FAUSTUS

And so will I ; let ruin
Roar like a cataract and drown the world !
Knowledge, begone ! All part and lot in Eve
I here renounce. Thou, Mephistopheles,
Serpent of Eden, take thy curse again,
Undo the sin of Adam, turn the years
Back to their primal innocence. By thine oath
Sworn in the mouth of hell, and by the power
Of all my magical art, I do command thee !

MEPHISTOPHELES

Softly, softly. What a hurry you are in ! You impetuous
young lovers want everything done in a moment. Take
away the knowledge of good and evil ? That's rather an
unusual order.

FAUSTUS

Can it be done, or no ?

MEPHISTOPHELES

Oh, it can be *done*. Everything can be *done*. But we have to charge a price for that sort of thing.

FAUSTUS

Quick. Name it. What price ?

MEPHISTOPHELES

The usual price. Your soul.

FAUSTUS

Take it. Sin and soul together.

MEPHISTOPHELES

And we can't sell you eternal youth upon freehold. I could manage a twenty-four years' lease if that would suit you.

FAUSTUS

It would be worth it, were it twenty-four hours or twenty-four minutes.

MEPHISTOPHELES

Very well. It's a bargain. (*Calling off towards Hell-mouth.*) Ho, there ! Bring me the bond.

[HELEN *vanishes, the stage darkens.*

Drawn in the name of John Faustus and of me, Mephistopheles. He to abjure and renounce the worship and service of God, and to enjoy in exchange eternal youth and primal innocence for four-and-twenty years ; at the end of which term he, the said John Faustus, shall become forfeit to the Devil, and be carried away, soul and spirit, body and bones, to Hell.

FAUSTUS

Quickly ! Where is Helen gone ? The air grows thick. My senses swim. The walls of Rome swoon into darkness about me.

MEPHISTOPHELES

Walls of Rome ? Nonsense ! You are in your own study at Wittenberg. See ! There are the lit candles (*the candles*

80

on the walls are lit). And your magic mirror *(the mirror becomes luminous).* And your servants about you.

[WAGNER *and* LISA *creep in to stand beside* FAUSTUS.

FAUSTUS

Where is the bond ? I will sign it with my blood.

WAGNER

Master, think again.

LISA

For thy dear soul's sake, take Christ's way, not this way.
 [*The image of* HELEN *is seen in the mirror.*

FAUSTUS

I come, I come, sweet Helen. Mephistopheles ! The bond !
Make haste.

[*Hell-mouth opens. Enter a* DEVIL *with the bond.*

MEPHISTOPHELES

It is here.

FAUSTUS

A pen—give me a pen. Where is the table ?

MEPHISTOPHELES

Here.

 [*Two* DEVILS *enter, bearing a board, which they offer to*
FAUSTUS, *kneeling, as though for a table.*

Pluck forth thy dagger. Prick thine arm. Write.

 [FAUSTUS *pricks his arm.* MEPHISTOPHELES *puts the pen into*
his hand.

FAUSTUS

See how the red stream runs upon the table like letters
written in fire. *Homo, fuge*—Flee, O man. What, shall I
turn back now ? (*Thunder.*) A dreadful voice cries in my
ear : Flee from the wrath to come ! O, whither shall I fly ?

LISA

Fly to the arms of God.

FAUSTUS

To the arms of love. Sweet Helen, receive my soul. (*He signs the bond. Thunder again.*) So, it is done.

MEPHISTOPHELES

Done ! And so clap hands on the bargain. (*Diabolic laughter.* MEPHISTOPHELES *tosses the bond to the* DEVIL, *who returns with it to Hell. Hell-mouth shuts.*) Come now, go to thy Helen as a new-made man.

FAUSTUS

How now ? What wilt thou do to me ?

MEPHISTOPHELES (*leading him to the mirror, where the image of the* YOUNG FAUSTUS *now appears beside* HELEN)

Have courage, my master, my bold conjurer, my masterful great magician. See, it's as simple as walking through a mirror. In with you, in with you !

[MEPHISTOPHELES *pushes* FAUSTUS *before him into the mirror, and* HELEN *and the* YOUNG FAUSTUS *walk out of it.*

FAUSTUS

Oh, I am free !

YOUNG FAUSTUS

I am free ! Come, Helen, to my arms !

[*As* YOUNG FAUSTUS *embraces* HELEN *and carries her off, right,* MEPHISTOPHELES *carries away the old body of* FAUSTUS *behind the mirror, which grows dark.*

LISA

He has fled from us into a dream. He has left the world empty. I am afraid of this thing that looks with his eyes and speaks with his voice.

WAGNER

It is Faustus and not Faustus. A stranger—yet I feel as though I had known him a long time.

LISA

It is the shadow of an imagination. . . . How still the town is ! No stir of wheel or footfall; no chime of the clock; no watchman's voice.

WAGNER

And how dark ! but not with the darkness of night. It is like the dusk and silence that creep before an eclipse.

LISA

My sun is eclipsed for ever.

WAGNER

Poor Lisa ! I know by my own heart how sorrowful you must be.

LISA

And I know by mine how bitterly I have hurt you. Forgive me, Christopher. We cannot help ourselves.

WAGNER

Please don't trouble about me. It really isn't worth it. It was presumptuous of me to set my hopes so high. One must expect disappointment in this world. (*Stoutly.*) And you know I am very absent-minded. I shall quite often forget to be miserable.

LISA

Dear, good Christopher. What a comfort you are ! . . . I'm sorry. I feel so desolate. I can't help crying.

WAGNER

There, there !

[*He puts his arm round her and pats her shoulder consolingly.* MEPHISTOPHELES *slithers in and speaks in his ear.*

MEPHISTOPHELES

Christopher, Christopher ! Shall I bring her to your bed ?

WAGNER (*whisking round*)

What the devil ? . . .

EP

83

(LISA *sees* MEPHISTOPHELES *and springs away
with a faint shriek*)

So it's you again !

MEPHISTOPHELES

Clever lad ! Now's your chance. Say the word, and I'll
tumble her into your arms like a ripe plum.

WAGNER

Don't be disgusting.

MEPHISTOPHELES

Oh, but you want her, Christopher.

WAGNER

No, I don't. Not if she doesn't want me. You needn't think
she'd listen to you. Anything *you* brought me wouldn't be
Lisa at all, but something nasty in her shape. I know your
tricks by heart. They're all in the conjuring book.

LISA

What's he saying, Christopher ?

WAGNER

A lot of filthy nonsense. Don't mind him.

LISA

I've been thinking what to do. Since our dear master is
out of his mind, we must stay close to him and perhaps
find some way to restore him.

WAGNER

To be sure we will.

LISA

And we will try and do his work—help the poor and heal
the sick with the remedies he taught us. And when God
sees what we are doing, He will say: That is the real
Faustus; that's what he really meant to do. Faustus is still
doing good by his servants' hands.

WAGNER

I always said you were clever. I should never have thought of that.

LISA

So you see, our work will plead for our master's soul.

WAGNER

Of course it will.

MEPHISTOPHELES

You flatter yourselves. I can't understand how men can be such fools.

WAGNER

Very likely not. There's a great deal you can't understand, you nasty, ignorant, dirty-minded demon. So hold your tongue and be damned to you !

MEPHISTOPHELES (*going*)

That is a very superfluous wish. Good evening.

WAGNER

Hi ! Stop ! What have you done with Dr. Faustus ?

MEPHISTOPHELES (*airily*)

We are just starting on a grand tour of the world. The Duchess Helen accompanies us. You might call it a little honeymoon trip. Constantinople. The Pyramids. Morocco. Persia. The Caucasus. The Earthly Paradise. All carried out in first-class style; a chariot-de-luxe with six dragons——

WAGNER

You don't say so. Then you can saddle me a chimaera—two chimaeras; and see that one of them is trained to carry a lady.

MEPHISTOPHELES

Certainly, certainly. Shall I charge them to your account, or the Doctor's ?

WAGNER (*firmly*)

You will include transport and service under your all-in terms. Did you bring our baggage from Rome ?

MEPHISTOPHELES

I'm afraid it was overlooked in the hurry.

WAGNER

Then fetch it. At once. Do you hear, you lazy devil ?

MEPHISTOPHELES

Immediately.

[WAGNER'S *and* LISA's *baggage is wafted in from the direction of Rome. Noise of wheels and trampling, off, right.*

Excuse me, the chariot is at the door.

[MEPHISTOPHELES *hurries off, Mansion* 1.

WAGNER

Come, Lisa. Dry your eyes. Be brave. Needs must when the devil drives. (*Cracking of whips, with snorting and trampling off, right.*) There's no time to waste in virtuous foot-slogging. Come Heaven, come Hell, we'll follow our Master Faustus.

[*Exeunt* WAGNER *and* LISA, *Mansion* 1.

FAUSTUS (*off right*)

Stand back, there. Give them their heads.

WAGNER (*off right*)

Up with you, Lisa. My stirrup, Mephistopheles.

MEPHISTOPHELES (*off right*)

To the four winds—away !

[*The infernal cavalcade is heard to rise in the air and fly off.*

SCENE III (*Mansion* 2)

INNSBRÜCK—THE EMPEROR'S COURT

[*Enter from Heaven, the Angel* AZRAEL. *He turns, as though answering someone inside.*

AZRAEL

Yes, sir. Certainly, sir. No difficulty at all, sir. Everything is quite in order.

[*He comes down and on, left, and walks briskly across to Mansion 2, sorting a sheaf of papers as he goes. At the entrance to the Mansion, he bumps, in a preoccupied way, into* MEPHISTOPHELES *coming out, and apologises without looking at him.*

Sorry; my fault.

[*Exit into Mansion.*

MEPHISTOPHELES (*looking after him*)

Stuck-up snob ! Can't even recognise an old companion who's come down in the world. (*Coming down-stage; in the voice of an impatient man summoning a waiter.*) Demons ! demons ! . . . the service is getting very slack. . . . Oh, for Satan's sake, hurry up there !

[*Enter a* DEVIL, *right.*

The fool wants another job done. A trifle for the Empress. Flowers out of season with ripe fruit and blossom on the same branch. Fetch it and look sharp. . . . Where from ? How the devil should I know ? Try the Hesperides. (*Exit* DEVIL, *left;* MEPHISTOPHELES *sits down and registers fatigue.*) This is the worst term of hard labour I ever undertook. If my four-and-twenty years were not up to-night, I should go on strike.

[*Re-enter, Mansion 2,* AZRAEL, *with a baby in his arms.*

Good morning, my lord Azrael.

87

AZRAEL

Why, it's Mephistopheles ! Good morning. And how's the
world with you ? You're looking a little exhausted.

MEPHISTOPHELES

Yes, I dare say. What's that you've got there ? Contra-
band ?

AZRAEL

No, no. Nobody you've any claim on. A sweet and pious
soul, born anew as a little child into the Kingdom of our
Father. Do you want to see her papers? (MEPHISTOPHELES
extends his hand in grim silence.) Suspicious old devil, aren't
you ?

MEPHISTOPHELES (*examining papers*)

So that's who it is.

AZRAEL

One of your failures, Mephistopheles. Nothing for you
there at all. Not so much as a whiff of Purgatory fire.
Only a brief educational course in the heavenly kinder-
garten. Satisfied ?

MEPHISTOPHELES (*returning papers with a grunt*)

All right. Just as well. We're run off our hoofs already.
My client Faustus——

AZRAEL

Yes. You've been keeping our department pretty busy
too. We were working overtime to deal with all those poor
souls parted from their bodies at the battle of Pavia. That
was your show, wasn't it ?

MEPHISTOPHELES

And a damned good show, too. I had fifteen legions of
devils fighting on the Emperor's side, to say nothing of
a magical tempest and a great quantity of heavy artillery
forged in our own works. To-day, we propose to sack
Rome, with lavish accompaniments of loot, rape, and

88

carnage. All this, if you please, by the orders of Faustus, who was once so tender-hearted, he would rescue the fly from the spider. What do you think of that ?

AZRAEL

A truly remarkable exhibition of primal innocence.

MEPHISTOPHELES

Primal innocence ? Primitive brutishness. The fellow's grown mischievous as an ape, lecherous as a goat, giddy as a peacock, cruel as a cat, and currish as a cross-bred tyke. Since first man fell into sophistication I have found no way to ruin him so effective as his restoration to a state of nature.

AZRAEL

Indeed ? Most interesting.

MEPHISTOPHELES

It's the greatest discovery of the age. Though the work it entails is apt to be a little trying.

[*Enter* DEVIL, *left, with flowering and fruited branch. He hands it to* MEPHISTOPHELES *and exit.*

This kind of nonsense is merely trivial. But when Faustus takes a fancy to do vulgar conjuring tricks——

AZRAEL

Such as ?

MEPHISTOPHELES

Such as swallowing a load of hay and a span of horses ; or breaking off his own limbs and strewing them about the place like a dissipated daddy-long-legs ; or drawing wine from the table-top, to astonish a parcel of drunken louts in a beer-cellar—well ! I do feel the whole thing's rather *infra dig.*

AZRAEL (*amused*)

You are of Lucifer's household. Your professional pride must sustain you.

[MEPHISTOPHELES *gives a short, vexed laugh. Enter, from Mansion* 2, FAUSTUS, *in the body of his transformation, and* WAGNER *reading a book.* WAGNER *has aged considerably in the intervening twenty-four years.*

Here comes your master, all agog for fresh marvels.

FAUSTUS

Hey, Mephistopheles ! Why are you idling there ? How fare our troops ? Is the siege well begun ?

MEPHISTOPHELES

It is begun.

WAGNER (*sitting apart and reading abstractedly*)

Fumitory mingled with treacle, and tormentil, to allay the fever.

FAUSTUS

With what success ?

MEPHISTOPHELES

Already the walls of Rome totter at the blast of our cannon. By every gunner stands an able fiend to aim the shot and set hell-fire to the match. From the bottomless pit, our sappers delve their way deep below mine and counter-mine.

FAUSTUS

Ha !

WAGNER

Herb of grace is a mithridate to combat the plague.

MEPHISTOPHELES

The Emperor's army go to the assault as though the devil were in them.

FAUSTUS

So they ought, so they ought. What forces have you dispatched ?

90

MEPHISTOPHELES

Halphas, the mighty earl, strides like a stork before his six-and-twenty legions of the damned. And Salmack, lord of corruption, marquess of hell, whose throne is in the sepulchre; where his strokes light, the maggot and the worm make holiday.

WAGNER

Hoarhound, pimpernel and pellitory are good for stinking sores.

MEPHISTOPHELES

Procell, the strong duke, is there, with eight-and-forty legions; Haborim and Labolas and all the captains of destruction.

FAUSTUS

Brave, brave ! This news delights me. What joy can equal the swift tumult of war—shock of arms, shouting of men, crash of cannon, the whole world piled together pell-mell in a quick confusion ! We must behold it, Mephistopheles. The Emperor is coming. I have promised that thou wilt show him all manner of fine things in a vision.

AZRAEL

So. There will be more work for me and my people.

FAUSTUS

Who is that ? Send him away, Mephistopheles. I am afraid of him. The smell of death is upon his garments.

AZRAEL

I am Azrael, angel of the souls of the dead; and where war goes, I must follow.

FAUSTUS

Don't talk about death. I don't like it. What are you doing here ?

AZRAEL

I am carrying to Heaven a soul that once was dear to thee.

FAUSTUS

Whose soul ?

AZRAEL

Hast thou forgotten Lisa, the little maid that loved thee ?

FAUSTUS

Lisa ? Is Lisa dead ? Wagner, do you hear this ?

WAGNER (*quietly*)

I know it, master. She died in my arms but now.

FAUSTUS

What killed her ?

AZRAEL

She went in thy name into all the plague-stricken quarters of this city, nursing the sick with the skill that Faustus taught her, when Faustus felt pity for men. The sickness took her and she died, and her last prayer was for thee.

FAUSTUS

Alas, alas ! Poor Lisa. Oh, Wagner, I can never be happy again. Why am I so vexed and thwarted ? I gave all I had for happiness. I gave—what was it I gave ? I have forgotten . . . I only sought to be happy, and how can I be happy now that Lisa is gone ?

WAGNER

She brought happiness to all who knew her, and that was her happiness and mine.

MEPHISTOPHELES (*to* WAGNER)

All the same, you would have done better to take my advice.

WAGNER

Art thou an authority upon happiness, thou shadow of an immortal grief? Master, I was never wise; but age and time have instructed me. To aim at happiness is to miss the mark; for happiness is not an end at all. It is something that comes of itself, when we are busy about other matters.

FAUSTUS (*without heeding him*)

Poor, pretty Lisa. She was kind to me. She looked after all my wants. What will become of me now?

AZRAEL

Thou wilt go to thine own place, Faustus. But her place is with the angels in Heaven.

[*Exit up to Heaven.*

WAGNER (*suddenly recalled to himself*)

I must work, I must work. So much to do, and so little time, now that I am all alone to do it. (*He wanders away, right, reading his book.*) Yarrow for green wounds; masterwort is a sovereign remedy for all diseases. . . .

[*He sits down and remains, absorbed in his studies.*

FAUSTUS (*inconsolably*)

My heart is broken. Nothing is left in all the world but sorrow. (*His eye lights on the branch* MEPHISTOPHELES *is holding, and his wandering fancy flits off in a new direction.*) That's pretty. What is it?

MEPHISTOPHELES

Surely you remember. It is the present you wanted to give to the Empress.

FAUSTUS

Oh, the Empress? She will be here presently. Hark'ee, Mephistopheles, the Empress is a fair woman, a blithe and buxom lady. She must be mine, d'ye hear me? I must and will possess her. Thou shalt bring her to me to-morrow.

MEPHISTOPHELES

To-morrow?

FAUSTUS

Yes, to be sure. I say, thou shalt bring her to-morrow.

MEPHISTOPHELES

There will be no to-morrow for you, master.

FAUSTUS

What's that?

MEPHISTOPHELES

Must I remind you of the terms of our bargain? I have served you diligently these four-and-twenty years. To-night the compact ends.

FAUSTUS

What then, devil, what then?

MEPHISTOPHELES

Why then you must die, and be forfeit, body and soul, to hell.

FAUSTUS

Death and hell? Death and hell? Don't speak those words. They madden me. I'll not hear them.

MEPHISTOPHELES

Stop your ears and welcome. But die you must and be damned.

FAUSTUS

Never believe it. There's no such thing as death, nor hell neither—save for a few such lubber-fiends as thou, to do the bidding of Faustus. Sin, death, age, sorrow—all that was a foolish dream, and fled like a dream for ever. Death comes with creaking bones and a sick carcase. Look at me, Mephistopheles. Have I aged a hair in four-and-twenty years? Not I. Then what's all this talk of death? It touches me not. I am the everlasting youth of the world.

94

I am John Faustus. (*Flourish without.*) Here comes the Emperor, with my lady the Empress. Give me that bough. Make haste.

[*Enter the* EMPEROR *and* EMPRESS, *attended.*

EMPEROR

Is Dr. Faustus of Wittenberg here in presence?

FAUSTUS

Good morrow and good fortune to your Imperial Majesties. Health, wealth and honour attend your Grace. And on you, most exquisite, beautiful and benign lady, may Venus bestow the plentitude of her favours. Be you ever fair and fruitful as this golden bough, fresh-plucked for your delight from the garden of the Earthly Paradise.

EMPRESS

Thanks, gentle doctor.

EMPEROR

We are much beholden to you. Tell us now. Is this promised spectacle ready, whereof you have reported such marvels?

MEPHISTOPHELES

Whenever you will. Command my master, and he shall command me.

EMPEROR

We know thee, Mephistopheles, as a cunning artificer and a spirit of great ingenuity. What are you able to show us?

FAUSTUS

Whatsoever you please to desire, of things near or far; past, present, or things to come.

EMPEROR

Then let us see and speak with Socrates, the wisest sage of antiquity.

EMPRESS

Oh, no ! Socrates was an elderly, ugly monster, with a snub nose and a scolding wife. Show us rather Adonis; or Apollo singing to his lyre, and attended by the nine Muses.

EMPEROR

Nay, madam; I am neither Adonis nor Apollo. Would you make a jealous husband of me ?

EMPRESS

Give me leave, I pray you. Indeed, my good lord, I insist.

EMPEROR

Do you so ? Then will I demand to look upon fair Helen of Troy, whose beauty set fire to the world. That is a fair revenge, is it not, Dr. Faustus ?

FAUSTUS

Your Majesty is more beautiful than ever Helen was.

EMPRESS

Fie, fie, sir. The flattery is too gross.

MEPHISTOPHELES

The truth is, madam, that by a delicate sorcery my master hath had the fair Helen to his paramour. But he grew weary and left her twenty years since, and now has no value for her.

FAUSTUS

Value ? What does that mean ? Helen was a troublesome baggage.

MEPHISTOPHELES

Man's delight is ever in the unattainable. When he is innocent, he longs for knowledge; when he is grown wise, he hankers after innocence. Between Lilith and Eve, Adam is unfaithful to both, and there is no contenting him.

FAUSTUS (*suddenly aggressive*)
But, mark you, Helen is mine for all that.

EMPEROR
We would not for the world offend you. Say no more.

MEPHISTOPHELES
Yet your Majesty shall have his will; for every man is
fated, once at least in his life, to look on Helen.

WAGNER
Plantain or rosa solis—what herb shall we lay to a
corroding ulcer ?

EMPEROR
Enough. We will think upon some other device.

EMPRESS
Do you choose, my lord. But I will not hear of Socrates or
Diogenes, or any such old, crabbed philosopher.

EMPEROR
Why then, since I am Emperor and hold half the world in
fee, let me see Alexander the Great, weeping because he
had no more worlds to conquer.

FAUSTUS
Tush, these are trifles. Alexander is dead and his con-
quests forgotten. I have better than that to show you.
    [*Enter a* SECRETARY OF STATE, *with a letter.*

EMPEROR
Anything, so it be diverting. (*To the* SECRETARY.) How
now ?

SECRETARY
Here is urgent news, sire, from Rome. Your Imperial
armies, leagued with the Constable of Bourbon, have this
night attacked the city, with intent to seize the Vatican
and overthrow the Pope.
    [*Sensation.*

EMPEROR

To overthrow the Pope?

EMPRESS

Alas! this is sacrilege!

EMPEROR

How came the news so soon?

FAUSTUS (*eagerly*)

Sire, this is what we would show you. My couriers, sped
by a magical device, have brought the message on the
wings of the wind. My arms, my arts are at your service.
We shall have as merry a battle as ever we had at Pavia.

EMPEROR

This will not do. Who writes the letter?

SECRETARY

The captain of your lanskers.

EMPEROR

Read what he says.

SECRETARY (*reads*)

"The Pope is the Emperor's worst enemy. This war is of
his making, and the insult to our master must be avenged.
For the honour of God he must be hanged, though I have
to do it with my own hand."

EMPRESS

Worse and worse.

EMPEROR (*as though persuading himself*)

True; the old fox has brought it upon himself. He has
intrigued against me with France, with Venice and with
Milan. He has roused up the Holy League to oppose me
—me, that have ever been the champion of the Church.
Nevertheless——

FAUSTUS

Why do you hesitate? Sweep him out of the way. You have the power—take all you can and keep it.

EMPEROR

We have never sought for conquest. Yet what is our own by right and inheritance we must and will defend.

MEPHISTOPHELES

Sire, if a poor ignorant devil may venture an opinion, there is but one question here. Who is to be master of Europe? Germany is yours; Spain and the Netherlands are yours. England is rotten with decay; she will truckle to the stronger power. France alone is your foe, and you cannot control France while your hands are tied by Rome. Crush the Pope and make Germany secure against France, and you may be sovereign of the world.

EMPEROR

Security? Yes. Chancellor, what do you say? The Pope is our spiritual sovereign?

CHANCELLOR

Then, sire, let him not meddle with the temporal arm. That belongs to Caesar, and the Emperor is Caesar's heir. The Church that appeals to Caesar's weapons is sold to Caesar already, and must abide the arbitration of Caesar.

MEPHISTOPHELES

Excellent, excellent. "Render unto Caesar——" I couldn't have quoted Scripture better myself.

EMPRESS

Yet how can we prevail, if God be not on our side?

WAGNER

Are we so sure that God takes sides? He sits in the centre like the sun and rules our orbits whether we will or no.

MEPHISTOPHELES

Well spoken, Wagner. God will not care, He makes His profit either way.

WAGNER

We may dwell on the light side or the dark side. That is all.

FAUSTUS (*contemptuously*)

Here's a wealth of my astronomy at second-hand.

EMPEROR

Right or wrong; if we attack the Pope the world will condemn us. And how then?

MEPHISTOPHELES

Use policy, sir, use policy.

FAUSTUS

I am weary of all this. Let's have the show.

MEPHISTOPHELES (*to* FAUSTUS)

Master, you are very right. (*To the* EMPEROR.) Say nothing, know nothing, watch how the battle goes. If your armies are defeated, hang your generals. If they are victorious, rebuke them in public and reward them secretly. Deny the deed and wink at it. Learn to be ignorant, for ignorance is the master-weapon of policy.

FAUSTUS

You are tedious with your policy.

MEPHISTOPHELES

As to the outcome of the fight, I will answer for it. Dr. Faustus will assist you by his art. (*Aside to the* CHANCELLOR.) And what better ally can you have in war than a profound scientific knowledge coupled with a total innocence of all moral responsibility?

CHANCELLOR

You may think such things, but not say them.

EMPEROR
There to the South, under the sun, lies Rome—
Would that the sun's rays, journeying hence, could show us
What his bright eye beholds !

FAUSTUS
                    Why, so they can,
My magical arts to aid.

WAGNER
                    The camomile
Was consecrate in Egypt to the sun;
It cureth ague and the melancholy.

MEPHISTOPHELES
Turn your back to the light, and look up northward,
Where the pale clouds lie like a silver screen.
See where the shadows waver, cast by the sun,
As spectres move on the Brocken.

EMPEROR
                    I see ! I see !

ATTENDANTS
O wonderful !

EMPEROR
                    The ramparts of a city—
The tumult of armed men—banners and lances—

FAUSTUS
Now they advance—now they retreat—the gunners
Stand to their cannon—

MEPHISTOPHELES
                    They touch the linstock now—

EMPEROR
The brazen mouths belch fire—

EMPRESS
              The smoke rolls over—

FAUSTUS
Up, winds, and send the echo ! Let us hear
The terrible voice, the glorious voice of war !
  [*Confused noise, and chambers shot off within.*

EMPEROR
The wall is breached ! Our lanskers storm the gap,
Crying, God save the Emperor !

CHANCELLOR
                    Stones and chains
Are hurled upon them !

FAUSTUS
                    Haro ! still they go forward—

SECRETARY
No, they give ground !

EMPRESS
                    Locked to and fro they sway—

EMPEROR
They are repulsed again.

CHANCELLOR
                    The town's defenders
Make sortie through the breach.

FAUSTUS
                        Now, now our hosts,
The hosts of hell stride out between the armies !

EMPEROR
A smother of smoke hides all.

102

FAUSTUS

They march, they march,
The tall, infernal seraphim ! O brave !
Raim, that once ruled as a throne in Heaven
Now like a raven spreads his sable pinions
And drives all backward.

MEPHISTOPHELES

Focalor the duke
On griffin wings hovers before the Romans,
And by his art calls up the inky Styx
Bubbling about their feet; bogs of delusion
Snare them about.

FAUSTUS

They stumble and go down
Held in the stinking marsh. The water drowns them !

EMPEROR

I see not this—only a mist of blackness
Shot through with flame.

CHANCELLOR

Ha ! the defenders rally !
Rank upon rank they crowd the wall. Our armies
Falter—

EMPEROR

The day is lost !

MEPHISTOPHELES

Strike, Halphas, strike,
Lord of the legions, builder and destroyer
Of towers !

[*A great explosion.*

FAUSTUS

Well done ! well done !

EMPEROR

A monstrous mine
Bursts in the breach, and blows them all to pieces !
Arms, bodies, stones and fragments, nightmare faces,
And shattered engines tumbled together, falling—

EMPRESS

O, fearful !

CHANCELLOR

In ! in ! in ! the town is taken !

EMPEROR

Our hosts rush on—they carry all before them—

FAUSTUS

Swords out and forward pikes ! The streets run blood,
The horses trample the fallen !

MEPHISTOPHELES

The Pope is fled
To the castle of Sant' Angelo—

EMPEROR

They surround him—

FAUSTUS

Brands ! brands ! and fire in the city !

EMPRESS (*covering her eyes*)

Enough ! no more !

MEPHISTOPHELES

Visions away ! The Emperor's arms prevail.

CHANCELLOR

Congratulations to your Majesty;
You are master now of Europe.

FAUSTUS

Is the show ended ?
I was enjoying myself. Begin again.

MEPHISTOPHELES (*briskly*)

Nothing more is needed. Your Majesty knows exactly where you stand. Write quickly now to your general, forbidding him to attack, and to all your brother sovereigns, explaining that the thing was done without your knowledge.

EMPEROR (*to* SECRETARY)

Put the letters in hand immediately.

MEPHISTOPHELES (*aside*)

Innocence and ignorance, most ravishing and blessed qualities, what should we do without you? If we have not set Europe at odds for four hundred years, my name is not Mephistopheles.

EMPEROR

Will not the Pope take vengeance for this?

MEPHISTOPHELES

Never fear it. He is bound hand and foot. See where he stalks, a pallid phantom, the sport and puppet of Empire.

[*The Phantom of the* POPE *appears, led in chains by* DEVILS.

POPE

John Faustus! John Faustus!

FAUSTUS (*shrinking like a whipped cur*)

Touch me not. Spare me. Let me go.

MEPHISTOPHELES

Courage, master. He cannot harm you. . . . There was a Pope once, scourged Faustus to the heart. He carries the sting in his memory. . . . Up, I say! What are you grovelling for?

POPE

Thou fool! This night shall thy soul be required of thee.

[*The* PHANTOMS *pass away.*

FAUSTUS (*laughing wildly*)

Aha ! did you hear that ? The old fool dares to threaten me ! Punish him, Mephistopheles ! Away, old rogue ! I will have you beaten, tortured, smothered in sulphur ! Up, devils, and after him !

MEPHISTOPHELES

Master, be quiet.

EMPRESS

Poor soul ! he is distracted.

MEPHISTOPHELES

Leave him to me. (*He shakes* FAUSTUS *into subjection as one would shake a dog.*) Come now. What will your friends think of you ? Never mind the Pope. (FAUSTUS *growls angrily at the name.*) I say, be quiet. Never mind him. (*To the* EMPRESS.) Fear nothing, madam. This fit takes him at times, but his bark is worse than his bite. (*To* FAUSTUS.) Peace, now. Consider. Is there no other entertainment we can show the Emperor ? Some handsome compliment ? Some pageant of victory ?

FAUSTUS (*all eagerness*)

Yes, yes. I am ready. What would your Majesty like to see ?

MEPHISTOPHELES

Master, we will show him the thing he asked for, the longing of his inmost heart. Music, strike up !

[*Music plays.*

The sun is fled, and darkness folds the earth
Like the chill shade that steals before the eclipse.

[WAGNER *springs to his feet, dropping his book with a crash.*

Rise up, thou star of evening, called by night
Hesperus, but in the morning, Lucifer,
And sometimes Venus, lady of love.

106

WAGNER
O master,
Look to thy soul, the sands are all run out.
[*Enter the vision of* HELEN, *veiled and carrying a wreath of laurel.*

EMPEROR (*rising*)
What wondrous shape is this, that gliding moves
So like a goddess, and in her hand holds forth
The glittering laurel ?

MEPHISTOPHELES
Learn and mark well her name.
She is all things to all men; and unto thee
The spirit of power, that like the will o' the wisp
Flits on the waters of time, and lures men on
To victory or to death. She is the promise
Of golden phantasy, the worm in the brain,
The song in the soul; she is the world's desire.
Gaze on her face, for men have died for her,
Great cities perished, gallant ships gone down,
Thrones and dynasties crumbled away to dust
For a glance of her eye. She is the unattained,
The unattainable.

HELEN (*standing high in the* EMPEROR'S *seat*)
Crowns for the victor, crowns,
Riches and wisdom, honour and glory and blessing.

EMPEROR
O, my heart burns. Unveil, thou wonder of women.

WAGNER
Beware, beware ! It is glamour !

MEPHISTOPHELES (*throwing back* HELEN'S *veil*)
Have thy will.
Behold the face of Helen.

107

FAUSTUS (*as the* EMPEROR *springs forward*)
Keep off ! She is mine !

EMPEROR
Stand back and let me not !

WAGNER
Master, forbear !
[FAUSTUS *throws* WAGNER *down. Exit* MEPHISTOPHELES,
back.

EMPEROR
Give place, I say !

EMPRESS
O Heaven !

FAUSTUS (*drawing his sword*)
Look to thyself !

CHANCELLOR
Will you lay hand upon the Emperor ?
Treason ! treason !
[CROWD *rushes in and surrounds them. In the confusion,*
HELEN *is carried up backstage by the* EMPEROR *and the*
CHANCELLOR, *and held in one of the entrances, with her back
to the audience. As she goes, she drops the laurel wreath near*
WAGNER. EMPRESS *in the arms of her ladies, left.*

A COURTIER
Vile sorcerer !

SECRETARY
Murderous dog !

CROWD
Down with him ! Down !

FAUSTUS
Help, Mephistopheles !
[*His cry momentarily arrests the action.* MEPHISTOPHELES
re-appears above Hell-mouth, right, flourishing the bond.

108

MEPHISTOPHELES

Faustus, the four-and-twenty years are past,
My service done. The devil claims his own.

FAUSTUS

Hell and damnation !
[*He is dragged down upon the forestage.* AZRAEL *comes down out of Heaven and enters, left, bearing a black pall.*
                    Wagner ! Lisa ! Christ !
Save me ! Have pity !

CROWD
Strike now !

MEPHISTOPHELES
                    · Bondsman of hell,
Die and be damned !

CROWD
Take that !

FAUSTUS
                    O I am slain !
[*As* FAUSTUS *falls among the crowd, there is a loud cry upstage.*

EMPEROR

She's fled ! Helen is vanished ! Melted away
Clean from our hands—only her garments left!
O sorcery !
[*He comes down a little, holding* HELEN'S *cloak.*

AZRAEL (*he is now on the forestage, with his back to the audience, and holding the pall spread out*)
                    Princes and earthly powers
Pass like a pageant, and make room for death.
Cover the face of Faustus.

[AZRAEL *and* WAGNER *cover* FAUSTUS *with the pall, and* AZRAEL *kneels beside the body, still with his back to the audience.*

109

WAGNER (*rising*)
O dear master,
Now art thou gone to find reality.
May God remember all thy willing manhood,
Not thy refusal. This thy golden dream
Shall dwell with me; and I will be thine heir,
Hoping that hope may yet outdo despair.
[*Exit* WAGNER *carrying the laurel wreath. The stage empties
of all except* AZRAEL *and* MEPHISTOPHELES, *who now comes
down.*

MEPHISTOPHELES
Thank you, Azrael. I will trouble you for that soul. You
needn't think you can sneak off with it. I saw you. It's
bought and paid for. Here is the bond. Be good enough to
hand it over.

AZRAEL (*who has the soul of* FAUSTUS *in his arms,
concealed in a bag*)
Just a moment. Things must be done in an orderly way.
The man is dead, and I have taken his soul in charge.
That is my office. If you think you have any claim on the
property, produce your evidence.

MEPHISTOPHELES (*producing the bond*)
There you are. Laugh that off.

AZRAEL
It appears to be properly executed. Always supposing
your client's soul was his to sell.

MEPHISTOPHELES
And whose else should it be?

AZRAEL
God's, Who redeemed it.

110

MEPHISTOPHELES

Nonsense. You can't get away with a legal quibble like that. The deed's watertight, and you know it.

AZRAEL

Well, you can take the soul on the security of the bond. But I shall enter a caveat, and appeal to the High Court.

[*He hands the bag over.*

MEPHISTOPHELES

You can enter anything you like. Come now, my little master, my high-and-mighty magician, let's have a look at you. You've given me trouble enough. Let's see how you like it when *I'm* the master! Believe me, my friend, I'll make it hot for you. (*He opens the bag and pulls out a* BLACK DOG.) Here! What's this? What's happened to it? You rascally, cogging angel! You cozening celestial sharp and shyster! This isn't the right soul!

AZRAEL

It's all the soul he's got.

MEPHISTOPHELES

It's a fraud! I've been tricked! That damned charlatan Faustus has cheated me. What's the use of a thing like this?

AZRAEL

That's your affair. *Caveat emptor.*

MEPHISTOPHELES

It was a perfectly good soul when I bought it. And now, look at it!

AZRAEL

It does seem to be rather out of repair. What have you been doing to it?

MEPHISTOPHELES

Great Lucifer! I like that. *I* been doing to it?

111

AZRAEL

You've had it these twenty-four years. If that's the way you treat the King's property——

MEPHISTOPHELES

I'll not stand it. God never plays fair. But I've got a clear case. I'll have the law of you——

AZRAEL

I'll sue you for damages——

MEPHISTOPHELES

I'll have my rights, I tell you. I will have justice !

[*Without pause or shift of furniture, the action passes to the next Scene.*

SCENE IV

THE COURT OF HEAVEN

[Heaven opens, and the JUDGE *appears above.*

JUDGE

Who calls on justice ?

MEPHISTOPHELES
                    I, Mephistopheles.
I am defrauded of my rightful due,
Payment for four-and-twenty years of hard
Devoted, scrupulous, vigorous, swift, exacting,
Skilled and assiduous labour, by John Faustus
The conjurer of Wittenberg, and this
Smug-faced angel of yours.

AZRAEL
                    Sir, I protest !
The fraud is all the other way. This fellow
Contracted with John Faustus for his soul,
Payable in exchange for value received,
The bond, post-dated, falling due to-day;
Which soul, I took in charge at Faustus' death
In execution of my official duty,
Lock, stock and barrel as it stood. He claimed
The same upon his bond, which seemed in order
So far as such things go. I handed over
The goods to him, entering a caveat
In the King's name, as to the ownership,
Since it might well appear the vendor had
No title to give, barter, sell, exchange,
Mortgage or pawn or otherwise dispose of
Crown property. Well and good. But in the interim
(To wit, the four-and-twenty years expired)
This Mephistopheles, by his own act——

113

MEPHISTOPHELES

That I deny. It was the act of Faustus
Or Azrael, or God, or all of them——

AZRAEL

Had so deformed the soul that it is useless
To God or him, Faustus or any one.
Therefore he claims: and first, against myself
That I did not deliver the true soul
But something substituted; or if I did,
Then against Faustus, for a wilful damage
Executed upon the soul, whereby
He should escape the explicit provision
Made by the bond; lastly, against the Crown,
That if it prove that Faustus or myself
Were acting in this matter as the King's agent,
The Crown may quit the claim. To all of which
I answer by a counter-claim for damage
Done to the goods by Mephistopheles—
A wrong to Faustus, and a clear offence
Against God's peace, His crown and dignity.

JUDGE

Set up my chair of justice in the court
Below there; I will give the cause prompt hearing.

[*The* JUDGE *comes down.*

MEPHISTOPHELES

Olimoth ! Belimoth ! (*To* AZRAEL.) Don't you trouble, sir,
I'll see to this. Lymeck ! Bealphares !

[*Enter* DEVILS *both sides.*

A seat for Justice !

[*Exeunt* DEVILS *and re-enter with a chair, etc.*

(*To* AZRAEL.)   This is nothing at all
To all the fetching and carrying, running about,
Materialising and dematerialising

114

This and that and the other, I've had to do
For Faustus—and of all the troublesome clients
Commend me to him.

[*The* JUDGE *enters.*

Pray, sir, take your seat.
There is the body of the said John Faustus,
This is the bond, and this the soul in question.

[*When the* JUDGE *has inspected the* SOUL, *the* DEVILS *take it
into the wings.*

JUDGE

Show me the paper.

MEPHISTOPHELES

Here. (*Fussily.*) You see it says
" I give my soul "—and " soul " in that connection
Must mean a human soul. I have been in business
Upon this planet several million years,
And it is always so interpreted.
But this alleged——

JUDGE

Stop talking, Mephistopheles.
Give me a moment to peruse the terms.
Why ! What is this ? " Agree to take away
The knowledge of good and evil ? " Come now, my poor
Deluded and benighted imp of darkness,
What did you think would happen to the soul
When you did that to it ?

MEPHISTOPHELES

I did not know;
How should I ? Never before, in all my long,
Industrious, strictly dishonourable career,
Have I been put to such a task as that.
It was hard work, but still, I did it.

GP

JUDGE
                    Yes;
Your zeal is your undoing. If I say
" Here is a sword of steel; I give it you
On one condition—that you treat it first
With the most powerful corrosive known
To alchemy "—what will the sword be like
By the time you claim it ?

MEPHISTOPHELES
                    Well, but if in good faith
I take and treat the sword as you require,
Not knowing how corrosive acts on steel,
Which yet you knew before you gave the order,
Is that an honest bargain ?

AZRAEL
                    And suppose
The sword was borrowed, and belongs in fact
To the armoury of God, what will God say ?

JUDGE
You have been swindled, Mephistopheles,
By accident, or by design, your own
Contributory negligence assisting.
Where were your wits ? 'Tis true, the foes of God
Are not at any time remarkable
For logic or for common-sense. However,
There must be justice; and the point you urge,
Azrael, is well taken, since all souls
Are God's indeed. Therefore these charges come
To rest on Faustus, who to you, and you,
And to God chiefly, is responsible.
We'll hear the prisoner in his own defence.

MEPHISTOPHELES
Faustus hath made himself into a beast
And has no wit to answer more than a beast.

Truly; but since, in this high court of Heaven
Where time is not, the present, past and future
Are all as one, and answerable together
Eternally to Him that is eternal,
I call the prisoner. Wake, thou that sleepest !
Not as thou art, but as thou wast, John Faustus,
Rise up and answer at the bar of judgment.

[*They take away the pall.* FAUSTUS *wakes in his own body.*

FAUSTUS (*as one dreaming*)
Whither away, love ? O return, return !

MEPHISTOPHELES
What ? Dreaming still on Helen ?

FAUSTUS
                              Christ ! Christ ! Christ !
They have taken away my Lord these many years,
And I know not where they have laid Him. Sir, if you
    know,
Tell me, for I denied Him, and just now
I heard the crowing of the cock. How long
The night has been ! And now the dawn is red
And a great storm coming . . . Hush ! for I remember.
I bartered away my soul for ignorance,
In ignorance, not knowing what I did.
There has been cheating somewhere. I was not happy
Those four-and-twenty years. Something was lost
That makes for happiness. Yet I seemed to know
Pleasure of a sort, and pain too—but they slipped
Like water through my fingers, neither perceived
Fully, nor remembered fully, nor assessed
At any quotable value.

JUDGE

Value exists
Not in the object, but the valuing mind;
The soul's choice makes the value. Therefore ask
This poor brute soul thou madest for thyself
How it doth reckon value.

[*Here a* DEVIL *shall show* FAUSTUS *the* SOUL *and retire again.*

FAUSTUS

I was cheated;
I did not bargain for a soul like this,
But for the primal innocence that was Adam's
Before he fell to knowledge. Is it sin
To cancel out a sin? Does God love sin
To set such value on it? Or is He helpless
To undo the past; and did the devil speak truth?

JUDGE

All things God can do, but this thing He will not:
Unbind the chain of cause and consequence,
Or speed time's arrow backward. When man chose
To know like God, he also chose to be
Judged by God's values. Adam sinned, indeed,
And with him all mankind; and from that sin
God wrought a nobler virtue out for Adam,
And with him, all mankind. No soul can 'scape
That universal kinship and remain
Human—no man; not even God made man.
He, when He hung upon the fatal tree,
Felt all the passion of the world pierce through Him,
Nor shirked one moment of the ineluctable
Load of the years; but from the griefs of time
Wrought out the splendour of His eternity.
There is no waste with God; He cancels nothing
But redeems all.

FAUSTUS (*to* MEPHISTOPHELES)
Serpent, thou didst deceive me !

MEPHISTOPHELES

So Adam said, and Eve; but I spoke truth
To them and thee. I warned thee that the truth
Would but beguile thee, as it beguiles all fools.
Thou askedst, What was I ? and I spoke truth;
And who made evil ? and I spoke the truth;
And what God was ? and there I turned the question
Back upon thee, and thou didst answer it
According to thine own folly; but I spoke truth.

JUDGE

The truth, but not the whole truth, Mephistopheles.
The whole truth is the perfect sphere of Heaven;
The hollow half-truth is the empty dome
That roofs the hall of hell, mocking with echoing
Shards of distorted speech and the fiends' laughter.

MEPHISTOPHELES

Laughter ! I tell you I have split my sides !
These wiseacres, that are too clever to see
A plain fact in broad daylight. Up they come,
Sidling and bridling like a fretful horse,
Showing the white of the eye. " What, that a fact,
That tall, black, ugly fence ? It can't be true,
There must be some way round—the gate, if you please."
And I am there—Oh, I am always there
To bow, and touch my hat, and take my fee
And open the gate that leads them into the circle,
The ring with the barriers, the closed ring, the place
From which there is no way, no way, no way out.
119

FAUSTUS

Love would have found the way, if way there were:
" Father, if it be possible, let this cup
Pass from Me." But it was not possible, never
Has been nor will be possible. Over the fence
Is the only road. For all the by-ways run
Down to the circle, the closed circle of self
From which there is no way out.

JUDGE
There is no way out.

MEPHISTOPHELES (*sings*)
Jump little man,
As high as you can;
The way across
Is by thorn and cross;
But the only way round
Leads into the pound,
So hey, so ho,
And over you go.

AZRAEL

You are too noisy. Silence in the court.
The prisoner waits for judgment.

MEPHISTOPHELES
Yes, and I
Wait for my fee, which has been tampered with.
Here is the bond: " I, Faustus, give my soul
For such and such considerations "—all
Duly fulfilled by me; but where's the soul ?
That thing there, which you flatter by the name,
I have no use for; it is not as specified.
If there is justice in this court at all
The devil must have his due.

JUDGE (*to* FAUSTUS)

                  You hear the charge
Preferred against you, on two counts. Imprimis:
That you did sell a soul for which Christ died;
A crime against God's crown. Next, that the price,
Promised in God's true gold, was paid in fact
With coin debased and worthless; a civil trespass
Against this gentleman. What have you to say?

FAUSTUS

I must admit the trespass, and the crime
That caused the trespass. I have no defence
Save ignorance; yet ignorance was itself
The very prize for which the crime was done;
Nor yet is ignorance a defence in law.
Speak thou, O righteous judge, for I am silent.

JUDGE

Poor, empty vessel whence the wine was spilt,
What shall we do with thee? Listen to judgment.
For this last time, God gives thee back again
The power to choose, weighing the good and evil—
A fearful option; yet no other course
Can justice take, since here thou standest bound
In thine own blood, and no remorse of thine
Can raze one jot or tittle from the law.
Hear, then, the dread alternative of choice;
And first, wilt thou, with that dumb changeling soul,
Incapable alike of hell or heaven,
Wander for evermore between the worlds
Unblest, undamned, unknowing?

FAUSTUS

                  Nor blest nor damned?
Merciful God, what kind of doom is this?

121

JUDGE

A gentle doom; sorrow shall never touch thee,
Nor pain, nor any question vex thee more;
Yea, though thy loss be wider than the world,
Or than a thousand thousand worlds at once,
Thou shalt not feel nor know it.

FAUSTUS

O, what loss?

JUDGE

A loss beyond all loss: to live content
Eternally, and never look on God;
Never behold the wonder of His face
Fiery with victory, bright above the burning
Wings of the cherubim; never to hear the loud
Exultation of trumpets shatter the sky
For the Lamb's marriage-feast; nor drink the wine
Of God; nor feel the glad earth thrill to the tread
Of the tall, strong, unresting angels' feet;
Nor know the dream of desire, that is beyond
All happiness; nor ever more to find
Beauty in sunlight, or the flowery fields,
Or in man's heart; nor ever laugh again.

FAUSTUS

No, no, no, no!

JUDGE

Does ignorance not suffice thee?
Wilt thou have knowledge after all, John Faustus?
Take back thy soul, then, and fulfil the bond;
Go down with Mephistopheles to hell,
And through the bars of those relentless gates
Gaze on the glory of the Lord far off
And know that He is terrible and just.

FAUSTUS

No choice but this ?

JUDGE

No other choice at all.

FAUSTUS

Either to lose God and not know the loss,
Nor even to remember God exists;
Or see the glories that I may not share,
And in the sharp hell of a lost desire
Burn on unquenchably.

JUDGE

So stands the choice.

FAUSTUS

O lost, lost, either way !

MEPHISTOPHELES

Excuse my laughter;
Justice hath pinned thee now in a cleft stick.
Writhe, my good friend, my toad beneath the harrow;
'Twill serve thee little, but no matter—squirm
For my amusement. How do you like this game ?
You're playing with cogged dice, cully—all sides alike.
Lend me an angel, we'll toss for it; heads I win
And tails you lose. If you call " God ! " and win,
Then I win you; and if you lose the throw,
Then you lose God; why then, call " tails," and get
The tail of the dog there. Maybe this will teach you
To play chuck-farthing with your soul !

FAUSTUS

I stand
Between the devil and the deep seas of God
On a road that leads nowhither. This is strange—
The love of God urges my feet towards hell,
The devil that seeks to have me flings me back

Into God's arms. Are you two allies, then,
Playing into each other's hands, and grinning
Friendship across my frontiers? I will have
The truth of this, although the stink reek up
And blast the airs of Heaven! Thou, Mephistopheles,
Answer again, and this time all the truth,
Art thou God's henchman or His master? Speak!
Who made thee?

MEPHISTOPHELES
God, as the light makes the shadow.

FAUSTUS
Is God, then, evil?

MEPHISTOPHELES
God is only light,
And in the heart of the light, no shadow standeth,
Nor can I dwell within the light of Heaven
Where God is all.

FAUSTUS
What art thou, Mephistopheles?

MEPHISTOPHELES
I am the price that all things pay for being,
The shadow on the world, thrown by the world
Standing in its own light, which light God is.
So first, when matter was, I was called Change,
And next, when life began, I was called Pain,
And last, when knowledge was, I was called Evil;
Nothing myself, except to give a name
To these three values, Permanence, Pleasure, Good,
The Godward side of matter, life and knowledge.

FAUSTUS
Thus far, then, have I come to learn the truth
I taught my servant, many years ago:
" The sun can cast no shade; only the dark

Dead body of earth or moon can make eclipse
Of his perpetual radiance." Thus I told him,
Being blind to my own parable; but he,
Knowing no syllable of sun or moon,
Walked in the light of the true innocence
To the end I sought for. Pity my blindness, sir,
For His dear sake that healed the blind and cast
The devils out——

MEPHISTOPHELES

                    Hast thou learned nothing yet?
He'll not reverse the past. The past is here
And thou must answer it.

FAUSTUS

                    O, by the Name
And power of Him that harrowed hell——

MEPHISTOPHELES
                                        Thou fool!
Thou juggling sorcerer! Thinkest thou with those
Same words wherewith thou once did'st conjure me
To conjure justice?

FAUSTUS
                    Devil, thou didst speak truth,
And with thine own truth will I choke thee now
To the deep of thy false throat. Not in the words
Is power, but in the faith of him that speaks,
And in the person of the very Christ
In Whom stands all the meaning of creation.
Words? They are rags, tags, fluttering remnants blown
Along the winds of fancy; only in Him
Is neither variableness nor shadow of turning.
Sir, I beseech thee, as thou art all truth,
Answer me truly; in this desperate choice
What would God have me do?

JUDGE

       I may not tell thee.
Only the knowledge of the good and evil
Gained once by sin, by double sin rejected,
Restored again by grace, is granted thee
For guidance. Thou must choose and choose alone.

MEPHISTOPHELES

Why, this is better than a circus ! Round
And round again till you're giddy, faster and faster
Round the closed circle. I met you first in a circle——
You should know something of circles. You're well inside,
Dodging the ring-master there, with the hoop in his hand
And the lash at your heels. Faster and faster, Faustus,
Round and round, and then—the crack of the whip
And through the hoop you go. So, Faustus, choose
In the devil's name.

AZRAEL

     In the name of the most high God
Choose, Faustus, and for ever.

FAUSTUS

       I have chosen.
I will go down with Mephistopheles
To the nethermost pit of fire unquenchable
Where no hope is, and over the pathless gulf
Look up to God. Beyond that gulf I may
Never pass over, nor any saint nor angel
Descend to me. Nevertheless, I know
Whose feet can tread the fire as once the water,
And I will call upon Him out of the deep,
Out of the deep, O Lord.

JUDGE

      Art now so bold
To call down God, thou that aforetime didst
With cowardly conjurations call up devils ?

126

Then tell me: art thou able to be baptised
With Christ's most bitter baptism, or to drink
The cup that all His shuddering mortal flesh
Shrank from, yet drank, down to the dark dregs, driven
By the strong spirit?

FAUSTUS

I dare not say I am able.
Yet I say this: that nothing thou canst do
Shall threat me from the quest of Christ eternal.
Yea, though thou stand with thy keen sword made bare
To keep me from Him, and have at thy command
In ninefold rank the terrible hosts of Heaven,
Yet will I seek Him. If I go down to hell
He is there also; or if He stand without,
My hands shall batter against hell's brazen gates
Till the strong bars burst asunder and let Him in.
Then will I seize Him, then fall down before Him,
Cling to His garments, hold Him fast by the feet,
Cry in His ear, " I will not let Thee go
Except Thou bless me. Even the unjust judge
Heard the poor widow, and Thou shalt hear me!
Spare not Thy rod, for Thou hast borne the rod,
Quench not Thy fire, for Thou didst pass through fire,
Only be with me! "

MEPHISTOPHELES

This is brave indeed!

FAUSTUS

Mock me not, nothingness; I have found courage
In Him that never feared to look on sorrow,
And though He slay me, I will trust in Him.

MEPHISTOPHELES

Then, Faustus, thou art mine!
127

FAUSTUS
                    Thine here and now,
But wheresoever and whensoever, God's.
Sir, I am ready.
                    MEPHISTOPHELES
            Come on, my violent friend.

                    JUDGE
The kingdom of Heaven suffereth violence,
And violent men may take it by assault
In the last breach of despair. Thus all things come
To their own place at last, the tares to the burning
And the good grain to God.
  (*To* MEPHISTOPHELES.)   Thou hast claimed thine own,
It is thine. Burn it. Touch not my good grain,
I shall require it at thy hand some day;
And for thou knowest that thy time is short,
Be diligent.
                    MEPHISTOPHELES
            I'll warrant thee for that.
Open the gates there !
  [*Hell-mouth opens.*
                    JUDGE
                    Faustus, look on me;
Through the harsh mask of judgment read my soul,
And when I meet thee at the gates of hell,
Know me again.
                    FAUSTUS
            Slay me, but leave me not.

                    JUDGE
Lo ! I will never leave thee, nor forsake thee
Even to the world's end. Take him, Mephistopheles,
And purge him throughly, till he find himself,
As I have found him mine. God is not robbed;
And I will bring mine own as I did sometime
From the deep of the sea again.
                    128

FAUSTUS

From the deep of the sea.

[FAUSTUS *is led away by* MEPHISTOPHELES *to Hell,* AZRAEL *and the* DOG *accompanying him. The* JUDGE *goes up into Heaven.*

DEVILS (*below*)

Deep calleth unto deep with the noise of the cataracts.

AZRAEL

Out of the deep have I called unto Thee, O Lord; Lord, hear my voice.

DEVILS (*below*)

Sheol is naked before Him, and Abaddon hath no covering.

AZRAEL

O let Thine ears consider well the voice of my complaint.

DEVILS (*below*)

They lie in the hell like sheep, death gnaweth upon them; their beauty shall consume in the sepulchre.

AZRAEL

But God hath delivered my soul from the place of hell, for He shall receive me.

[*The* JUDGE *being now come up into Heaven, the gates are opened with a great light.* FAUSTUS *at Hell's mouth sees the glory of Heaven.*

ANGELS (*above*)

Return, return, O Shulamite; return, return, that we may look upon thee.

AZRAEL

If any man's work shall be burned, he shall suffer loss.

DEVILS (*below*)

Where their worm dieth not, and their fire is not quenched.

ANGELS (*above*)

But he himself shall be saved, yet so as by fire.

[FAUSTUS *follows* MEPHISTOPHELES *into Hell, and the* DOG *with him. Hell-mouth is shut upon them.*

CHORUS (*while* AZRAEL *returns into Heaven*)

Multitudes, multitudes in the valley of decision; for the day of the Lord is near in the valley of decision.

That which the palmer-worm hath left hath the locust eaten; and that which the locust hath left hath the canker-worm eaten.

A fire devoureth before them, and behind them a flame burneth.

Multitudes, multitudes, in the valley of decision.

Rend your heart and not your garments, and turn unto the Lord your God;

And I will restore unto you the years which the locust hath eaten.

Multitudes, multitudes—I beheld, and lo! a great multitude,

Ten thousand times ten thousand, and thousands of thousands.

Worthy is the Lamb that was slain to receive power, and riches, and wisdom, and strength, and honour, and glory, and blessing;

Blessing and honour, and glory, and power, be unto Him that sitteth upon the throne, and unto the Lamb, for ever and ever. Alleluia. Amen.

FINIS

THE DOROTHY L. SAYERS SOCIETY

THE DOROTHY L. SAYERS Society, with now some 500 members worldwide, was founded in her hometown of Witham in 1976. Its aims are educational: to collect and preserve archival material, to act as a centre of advice for scholars and researchers, and to present the name of Dorothy L. Sayers to the public by encouraging publication and performance of her works and by making grants and awards. We have close links with the Marion E. Wade Center at Wheaton College, Illinois, where the majority of her papers are held.

An annual Convention is held with at least half a dozen further meetings not only in UK, but we have also met in USA, Germany, Sweden, France and The Netherlands, studying themes ranging from Incunabula, fungal poisons and Dante, to Education and the Nicene Creed. We have held concerts of music, have sponsored performances of The Zeal of thy House in Canterbury Cathedral, the Bach B Minor Mass in Oxford, and new incidental music for our production of some of The Man Born to be King plays in London. 1993 saw the Centenary of the birth of Dorothy L. Sayers with over 30 events worldwide. Her poem "The Three Kings" was set as a carol, and performed and broadcast in the Midnight service at Canterbury Cathedral.

Our publications include the Poetry of Dorothy L. Sayers, five volumes of The Letters of Dorothy L. Sayers, and, most recently, two hitherto unpublished talks by DLS, Les origines du roman policier, and The Christ of the Creeds. We have extensive archives.

Witham now has a Dorothy L. Sayers Centre in the public library where we hold an annual Sayers Lecture and a statue of DLS with her cat Blitz.

Further information is available from the Society's headquarters at Rose Cottage, Malthouse Lane, Hurstpierpoint, West Sussex BN6 9JY or the web site: http://www.sayers.org.uk

Christopher Dean
DLS Society Chairman
2011

Made in the USA
Lexington, KY
05 November 2016